1 MONTH OF
FREE
READING

at

www.ForgottenBooks.com

By purchasing this book you are
eligible for one month membership to
ForgottenBooks.com, giving you
unlimited access to our entire
collection of over 1,000,000 titles via
our web site and mobile apps.

To claim your free month visit:

www.forgottenbooks.com/free891767

ISBN 978-0-266-80253-2
PIBN 10891767

Episcopal Churchwomen
Chapel of the Cross

Yearbook
1985-86

IN LOVING MEMORY

Kloe Marie K. Juers

Ann Eileen Elliott Weiss

Anne Goodwyn Boisseau Jones

Johanna Christine Andresen

Mary Lois Shoaf Slayton

Margaret Tebbetts Henderson

Freshteh Golkho

Virginia Cary Read

Rose Wade Scroggs Harvel

Julia Anthony Powell

Eleanor Harwood

Mildred Hall Wilkerson

Chapel of the Cross

AN EPISCOPAL PARISH

304 E FRANKLIN ST   CHAPEL HILL, NC 27514-1193   (919) 929-2193

THE REV STEPHEN I ELKINS-WILLIAMS
Rector

THE REV NANCY REYNOLDS PAGANO
Associate for Parish Ministry

THE REV DAVID D STANFORD
Associate for Campus Ministry

October 7, 1985

Dear Friends,

One of the major challenges facing a large, gifted parish is maintaining a sense of community strong enough to enable the parish, both as individuals and as a body, to "reach out in love and concern for others." (BCP, p. 429)   If our focus is too inward, we become too self-centered and self-satisfied and Christ is not served. If our energy is only directed outwards, we lose our sense of support and belonging, so that our efforts lose their strength, and Christ is not served.

The Episcopal Churchwomen, whose ministry is reflected in this yearbook, offer a model to the parish for keeping these two emphases in balance. By maintaining both a strong sense of community and one which is directed toward serving others, the E.C.W. adds immeasurably to the parish's living out of its call to minister both to its own people and to those beyond its bounds.

On behalf of the parish, I give thanks to God for the example and the ministry of the Episcopal Churchwomen. May God continue to make it fruitful.

Faithfully,

Stephen

Stephen J. Elkins-Williams

CONTENTS

EXECUTIVE BOARD OF THE EPISCOPAL CHURCHWOMEN
DIOCESE OF NORTH CAROLINA
1984-1985

President

Mrs John T Gregory (June)
5601 Westfield Drive
Greensboro, NC 27410
(919) 288-2161

Vice President

Mrs Edward B McKenzie (Nan)
2525.West Innes Street
Salisbury, NC 28144
(704) 633-2328

Secretary

Mrs. Robert G Darst (Carolyn)
3310 Starmount Drive
Greensboro, NC 27403
(919) 292-4008

Treasurer

Mrs Bruce Rinehart (Mary)
2944 St Andrew's Lane
Charlotte, NC 28205
(704) 377-0060

Treasurer-elect

Miss Alice Herring
204 Raleigh Road West
Wilson, NC 27893
(919) 243-2757

Secretary of Devotional Life

Mrs Conrad B Sturges (Harriette)
406 Spring Street
Louisburg, NC 27549
(919) 496-5272

Secretary of Christian Education

Mrs Thomas Droppers (Mary Ellen)
2600 Westmoreland Drive
Greensboro, NC 27408
(919) 288-9857

Secretary of Christian Social Ministries

Mrs Charles S Robbs (Wilda)
3315 Anderson Drive
Winston-Salem, NC 27107
(919) 788-8198

Secretary of Missions

Mrs. John B. Smith (Jean)
605 Minturn Avenue
Hamlet, NC 28345
(919) 582-1001

United Thank Offering Treasurer

Mrs Gerald Barrett (Phyllis)
P.O. Box 1343
1021 Laurel Hill Road
Chapel Hill, NC 27514
(919) 967-2153

Secretary of Christian Ministries
& College Work

Ms. Carol Reed (Carol)
P.O Box 21871
Greensboro, NC 27420
(919) 273-0907

Secretary of Promotion

Mrs. W Kimball Griffin (Lib)
3818 Somerset Drive
Durham, NC 27707
(919) 489-0536

Chairman of Altar Work

Mrs T E Hofler, Jr. (Mary)
1904 West Cone Boulevard
Greensboro, NC 27408
(919) 288-3245

Church Periodical Club Director

Mrs John T. Rice (Grace)
St. Mary's College
900 Hillsborough Street
Raleigh, NC 27603
(919) 821-7457

Yearbook Editor

Mrs Frank Meadows (Notie Vay)
104 Nottingham Court
Rocky Mount, NC 27801
(919) 443-1567

Executive Council Member

Mrs J Haywood Evans (Scott)
3818 Regent Road
Durham, NC 27707
(919) 489-2721

Immediate Past President (ex-officio)

Mrs D James Coleman, Jr (May)
800 Macon Place
Raleigh, NC 27609
(919) 787-2184

Special Committees:

Chairman of Working Women's Committee

Mrs William Partin (Shara)
1203 Willow Drive
Chapel Hill, NC 27514
(919) 942-4080

Christian Social Ministries Committee on
Women's Issues Representative.

Mrs Richard M Johnson (Carole)
502 Woodland Drive
Greensboro, NC 27408
(919) 273-1482

Chairman, Conference Center Altar Guild

Mrs W R Hashinger (Martha)
3204 Round Hill Road
Greensboro, NC 27408
(919) 288-7987

Convocation Chairmen:

Northeast

Mrs Bob White (Boo)
105 Nottingham Court
Rocky Mount, NC 27801
(919) 443-3220

Central

Mrs. Herbert Scoggin (Anne)
806 Woodland Trail
Louisburg, NC 27549
(919) 496-3758

Northwest

Mrs. Herbert W. Safriet (Marian)
P.O. Box 1222
Reidsville, NC 27320
(919) 432-1552

Southwest

Mrs Walter A. Reynolds (Sandra)
1966 Overhill Road
Charlotte,. NC 28211
(704) 366-5010

Sandhills

Mrs Allen J. Green (Betty)
Route 1, Box 10
Wagram, NC 28396
(919) 369-2746

5

COLLEGE CHAPLAINS

Harves, The Rev. Charles — Chaplain to the University of N C at Greensboro
930 Walker Avenue, Greensboro 27403 Tel.919-272-4672

St. Mary's College — 900 Hillsborough St.
Raleigh 27611. Tel. 919-828-2521, Ext. 222

Keese, Peter — Hospital Chaplain, Duke University Medical Center
Box 3112, Durham 27710. Tel. 919-684-3586 (Office)

Brill, The Rev. Gene — Chaplain to Duke University
Box 4844, Durham 27706 Tel. 919-286-0642

Brettman, The Rev. William — Chaplian to North Carolina State University
P.O. Box 5276, Raleigh 27650

DIOCESE OF NORTH CAROLINA

DIOCESAN HOUSE — 201 St. Alban's Drive, Raleigh
Telephone (919) 787-6313 — P. O. Box 17025
Zip 27619

Bishop . . . . The Rt. Rev. Robert W. Estill, D. Min.
Suffragan Bishop . . . . The Rt. Rev. Frank Vest
Director of Christian Social Ministries . . . . The Rev. Lex Mathews
Secretary . . . . The Rev. Carl F. Herman, Greensboro
Treasurer . . . . Mrs. Letty J. Magdanz
Historiographer . . . . Dr Lawrence F. London, Chapel Hill
Editor, *THE COMMUNICANT* . . . . Mr. John B. Justice
Chancellor . . . . Mr. Joseph Cheshire
Missioner to the Deaf . . . . The Rev. J. Barry Kramer
Program Director . . . . The Venerable Neff Powell

CONVOCATIONS

I. NORTHEAST	II. CENTRAL	III. NORTHWEST	IV. SOUTHWEST	V. SANDHILLS
Battleboro	Cary	Asheboro	Albemarle	Ansonville
Enfield	Chapel Hill	Burlington	Charlotte	Hamlet
Halifax	Durham	Eden	Cleveland	Laurinburg
Jackson	Erwin	Elkin	Concord	Pittsboro
Littleton	Fuquay-Varina	Germanton	Cooleemee	Rockingham
Northampton County	Garner	Greensboro	Davidson	Sanford
Ridgeway	Henderson	Haw River	Fork	Southern Pines
Roanoke Rapids	Hillsborough	High Point	Huntersville	Troy
Rocky Mount	Kittrell	Kernersville	Iredell County	Wadesboro
Scotland Neck	Louisburg	Lexington	Monroe	
Speed	Oxford	Mayodan	Salisbury	
Tarboro	Raleigh	Mount Airy	Statesville	
Warrenton	Roxboro	Reidsville	Woodleaf	
Weldon	Smithfield	Thomasville		
Wilson	Townsville	Walnut Cove		
	Wake Forest	Winston-Salem		
	Yanceyville			

6

CONVOCATION II-CENTRAL
Dean: The Rev. Robert C. Johnson, Jr.
1737 Hillandale Road
Durham 27705

Convocation Officers

Chairman..............Ann Scoggin (Mrs. Herbert P.), 806 Woodland Trail, Louisburg 27549
Vice Chairman & Sec.................Mrs. Adele B. Butts, 128 Nelson Street, Durham 27707
Treasurer.................Edith Woolard (Mrs. E.W.), 2911 Dogwood Drive, Henderson 27536

MISSIONARIES AFFILIATED WITH THE DIOCESE OF NORTH CAROLINA

BOESSER, THE REV. MARK, P O Box 995, Wasilla Alaska 990687
  Birthday-May 19
CHAPMAN, MRS HENRY, 1617 Hendersonville Rd , Asheville, NC 28803
  Birthday-July 13
FORTUNE, THE REV. JAMES, Rt. 3, Box 222c, Littleton, NC 27850
  Birthday-October 19
GORDON, JOCELYN, 607 Fraker Place, Eden, NC 27288
  Birthday-June 24
JONES, CATHERINE, S I M , B P 41, Maine-Sora, Niger Republic, West Africa
  Birthday-July 20
PEELE, STUART and EVERALL, Worldteam, Haiti, c/o MFI, Box 15665, West Palm Beach, Florida 33046
  Birthdays - Stuart, June 19 Everall, July 13
SIMMONDS, MRS HARVEY, Rt 4, Box 625, Lexington, NC 27292
  Birthday-Dec 25
TORREY, THE REV ARCHER and JANE, Jesus Abbey, Box 17, Tae Baek P O Kang Won Do 241-11, Korea
  Birthday-Archer, Jan. 19 Jane, Feb. 4
WOLFF, MISS RACHEL, 242 New Drive, Apt. B, Winston-Salem, NC 27103
  Birthday-Sept 19

Board of the Episcopal Churchwomen
Chapel of the Cross Branch 1985-86

President
Ele Fisher (Mrs. Mark)
400 Bowling Creek Road
Chapel Hill
929-9172

Vice-President
Barbara Schliebe (Mrs. Eric)
140 Stateside Drive
Chapel Hill
967-3070

Past President (ex officio)
Clare Baum (Mrs. Walter)
520 East Franklin Street
Chapel Hill
929-7817

Secretary
Rachael Long
20 Hayes Road
Chapel Hill
968-0412

Corresponding Secretary
Paula Meyer (Mrs. George)
1516 Arboretum Drive
Chapel Hill
967-7944

Treasurer
Marty Ensign
1214 Carol Woods
Chapel Hill
967-0019

Treasurer-Elect
Mudge Marsh
328 Forbush Mtn. Drive
Chapel Hill
929-8612

Secretary of Missions
Harriet Koch (Mrs. Robert J.)
159 Hamilton Road
Chapel Hill
967-4354

Secretary of Devotions
Mary Harris (Mrs. Tyndall)
P. O. Box 2533
Chapel Hill
489-7371

Secretary of Christian Social Ministry
Lynn Charlton (Mrs. John)
Rt. 2, Box 729
Chapel Hill
929-9202
and
Linn Alexander (Mrs. Macy)
413½ Pritchard Avenue
Chapel Hill
929-8136

Secretary of College Work and Christian
Ministries
Edie Poole (Mrs. Gary)
203-C Branson Street
Chapel Hill
933-6649

Secretary of Promotion
Lexie Simpson
#3 Penick Lane
Chapel Hill
929-4198

Chairman of the Altar Guild
Phyllis Barrett (Mrs. Gerald)
P. O. Box 1343
Chapel Hill
967-2153

Church Periodical Club Director
Anne Corpening
130 Carol Woods
Chapel Hill
942-8956

United Thank Offering Treasurer
Carolyn Powell (Mrs. Charles)
2446 Honeysuckle Road
Chapel Hill
929-3507

Secretary of Christian Education
Kathie Heffner (Mrs. Thomas)
103 Porter Place
Chapel Hill
929-4637

Vestry Liaison
Stephanie Willis (Mrs. Park)
403 Colony Woods Drive
Chapel Hill
967-5050

Special Area Chairmen
Episcopal Churchwomen
Chapel of the Cross 1985-86

Newcomers (ECW)
Paula Meyer (Mrs. George)
1516 Arboretum Drive
Chapel Hill
967-7944

Parishcare Liaison
Lisa Fischbeck
313 Granville Road
Chapel Hill
929-7267

Guild of the Christ Child
Denise Horn (Mrs. James)

and
Trisha Davis (Mrs. Bob)
132 Hunter's Ridge Road
Chapel Hill
929-6536
and
Josephine Floyd
175 Hamilton Road
Chapel Hill
967-7388
and
Anne Stapleton (Mrs. Jack)(Hand-Me-Down)
205 Gary Road
Carrboro 27510
942-8303
and
Mary Swank
Q-12 Kingswood Apts.
Chapel Hill
929-9627

Parliamentarian
Janet Devine (Mrs. John)
311 Old Forest Creek Drive
Chapel Hill
929-2424

Parish House Parlor
Mary Arthur Stoudemire (Mrs. Sterling)
712 Gimghoul Road
Chapel Hill
942-2468

Junior Choir
Mary Arthur Stoudemire
  (Mrs. Sterling)

Senior Choir and Clergy Vestments
Irene Rains
P. O. Box 306
Chapel Hill
942-1791
        and
Vivian Varner (Mrs. Barney)
294 Azalea Drive
Chapel Hill
933-6863

Newsletter Editor
Katherine Kopp (Mrs. Vincent)
738-A Gimghoul Road
Chapel Hill
933-8383

ABC Sale Chairman
To Be Announced

Yearbook
Katherine Kopp
        and
Pam McGaghie (Mrs. Bill)
112 East Village Lane
Chapel Hill
967-4430

ECW Luncheons
Marcy Ollis (Mrs. David)
2 Foxridge Road
Chapel Hill
968-4020

ECW Coffees
Diana Wallace (Mrs. Carl)
140 Carolina Forest
Chapel Hill
967-3693

9

Chapel of the Cross
304 East Franklin Street
929-2193

Clergy:

The Rev. Stephen J. Elkins-Williams, Rector
The Rev. David D. Stanford, Associate for Campus Ministry
The Rev. Nancy Reynolds Pagano, Associate for Parish Ministry

Priests Associate: the Rev. Dr. Richard W. Pfaff, the Rev. Dr. John H. Westerhoff, III
the Rev. Dr. Robert C. Gregg, the Rev. John A. Zunes, the Rev. Joseph P. Matthews

Music Program:

Dr. Wylie S. Quinn, III, Organist-Choirmaster.

Christian Education:

Diana Scholl, Christian Education Coordinator

Parish Office Staff:

Thomas A. Bloom--Office Manager
Allen Irvine--Parish Secretary: receptionist, appointments, and scheduling
Karen Lenchek--Parish Secretary: typing, printing, and data processing
Sandra Griffin (Mrs. Geoffrey)--Hospitality Coordinator
Nora Lewis--Bookkeeper
Doris Cotton (Mrs. Gattis)--Housekeeper
Joseph Horton--Sexton

CONSTITUTION AND BY-LAWS

EPISCOPAL CHURCHWOMEN, CHAPEL OF THE CROSS

CONSTITUTION

Article I
NAME

The name of this organization shall be "The Chapel of the Cross Branch Episcopal Churchwomen, Diocese of North Carolina."

Article II
PURPOSE

The purpose of this organization shall be to enable the women of the parish of the Chapel of the Cross through worship, study, service, and fellowship to share more fully in the mission of the whole Church

Article III
MEMBERSHIP AND MEETINGS

Section 1: The membership of this organization shall be composed of those women of the parish and community who share in its program.

Section 2: The Branch shall meet not less than four times a year.

ARTICLE IV
OFFICERS

Section 1: The elected officers of this organization shall be a President, a Vice-President, a Secretary, a Treasurer, and those officers needed to carry out the program of the Branch, such as a Secretary of Christian Education, a Secretary of Christian Social Ministries, a Secretary of Devotional Life, United Thank Offering Treasurer, a Secretary of Missions, a Secretary of College Work and Christian Ministries, a Secretary of Promotion, and a Church Periodical Club Director.

Section 2: The Executive Board shall consist of the elected officers and appointed officers. It shall meet not less than four times a year and also at the call of the President.

Section 3: The Executive Committee shall consist of the President, Vice-President, Treasurer, Secretary, and Chapter Chairmen (if there are any) and meet only at the call of the President.

Article V
DELEGATES TO ANNUAL MEETING

Delegates to the Annual Meeting of the Diocesan Episcopal Churchwomen shall be chosen by virtue of their office in the following order: President and President-elect. Alternates and any additional delegates to which the Branch is entitled are to be elected by the general membership.

Article VI
AMENDMENT

This constitution may be amended at any general meeting of the Branch by a two-thirds vote of the members present provided that a written copy of the proposed amendments shall be filed with the Branch Secretary and a copy mailed to every member at least one month prior to the date of voting.

BY-LAWS

Article I
ELECTION OF OFFICERS

The President shall appoint, and announce by January, a nominating committee who shall present at the February meeting a slate of one or more nominees for each office to be filled, and a slate of delegates and alternates to Annual Meeting. It is recommended that at least one past president be included on the nominating committee. The consent of the Nominees shall be obtained before their names are presented. Nominations for officers may be made from the floor at the March meeting, provided consent of nominees has been obtained before their names are presented.

Article II
TERM OF OFFICE

Section 1 The President and Vice-President shall be elected for a term of one year. All other Branch officers shall be elected for a term of two years. The President and Vice-President shall take office the same year. The Treasurer, Secretary of Christian Education, Secretary of Missions, and Secretary of Promotion will assume office in the same year, the Secretary, the Secretary of Devotional Life, United Thank Offering Treasurer, Secretary of Christian Social Ministries, and Secretary of College Work and Christian Ministries in alternate years.

The out-going President shall be ex officio member of the Board for the year following her term of office. The office of Treasurer shall have a one-year apprenticeship coinciding with the final year of office of the outgoing Treasurer prior to assuming the two-year office

Section 2 Newly elected officers shall be installed at the May meeting of the Branch.

Section 3: Out-going and newly installed officers shall attend a joint meeting of the Executive Board in May.

Section 4: Vacancies during the year shall be filled by the President. Unexpired terms shall be filled by the current nominating committee.

Article III
DUTIES OF THE EXECUTIVE BOARD AND THE EXECUTIVE COMMITTEE

Section 1. The Executive Board shall meet to consider suggested activities and business of the Episcopal Churchwomen and make recommendations to the Branch for its approval.

Section 2 The Executive Committee shall be empowered to act on emergency measures

Article IV
DUTIES OF OFFICERS

Section 1. Each elected officer should have the diocesan Episcopal Churchwomen Yearbook and refer to it frequently with special attention paid to the section pertaining to her work.

Section 2 The President shall have general oversight of all work of the Branch and shall appoint the chairmen of necessary committees. She shall preside at meetings of the Branch and of the Executive Board, and Executive Committee when necessary. She shall be an ex officio member of all committees. She shall make a report to the annual meeting of the parish when requested by the Rector.

Section 3 The Vice-President shall act in the absence of the President, and shall have specific duties to be decided in conference with the President

Section 4 The Secretary shall record the proceedings of the Branch, the Executive Board, and the Executive Committee. She shall carry on necessary correspondence, and see that past records are suitably filed at the parish house in the Cobb E C W Room.

Section 5 The Treasurer shall receive and disburse all money, except the United Thank Offering and Church Periodical Club funds, and shall make a detailed report at each meeting of the Branch. She shall send a pledge in December and an annual report in January to the Diocesan Treasurer. The treasurer's accounts shall be verified by a public auditor annually.

Section 6 A Secretary of Christian Education shall promote and stimulate Christian educational work in the Branch. She shall provide programs for Branch meetings

Section 7 A Secretary of Christian Social Ministries shall promote the Christian social relations in the parish and community. She shall be the representative of the Chapel of the Cross Branch of the Episcopal Churchwomen to the Chapel Hill Interfaith Council and Churchwomen United.

Section 8. The Treasurer of the United Thank Offering shall receive the U.T.O in the spring and fall of each year and shall remit it directly to the diocesan U.T.O Treasurer. She shall promote the program and the understanding of the United Thank Offering.

Section 9. The Secretary of Promotion shall be responsible for news of the E.C.W. in the local media, and for liaison with the Diocesan Secretary of Promotion.

Section 10: The Secretary of Missions shall stimulate interest in missions. She shall be responsible for sending birthday and Christmas remembrances to missionaries assigned to the Branch by the Diocesan Chairman of Missions. She shall remind the Branch Treasurer of the missionary Christmas gift which is to be sent to the proper receiver before November.

Section 11 The Secretary of College Work and Christian Ministries shall maintain contact with students of the parish who are away, work closely with the clergy and chaplain offering them her talents and time. She shall inform young women of the parish of the opportunities for full-time work in Christian ministry

11

Section 12: The _Director of the Church Periodical Club_ shall
know and understand the work of the C.P.C. which
provides reading material for those who could not
otherwise obtain it.

Section 13 All _Branch Officers_ shall keep notebooks which
outline duties and suggestions for the discharge
of their office These notebooks shall be given
to their successors at the joint Executive Board
meeting in May.

Article V
CHAPTERS

When it is deemed necessary for effective service,
the Branch may be divided into chapters or small
groups of special interests as long as the purpose
of the chapters/groups is consistent with the purpose of the Episcopal Churchwomen as stated in
Article II of the Constitution of this organization.

Article VI
FINANCES

Section 1   Finances and matters of business and policy shall be
discussed and decided only in meetings of the Branch.

Section 2.   Each member shall be given the opportunity to make a
pledge to the Branch. Pledges shall be collected by
the Branch Treasurer.

Section 3:   There shall be a Finance Committee consisting of the
President, Treasurer as chairman, and at least one
other member appointed by the President which shall
prepare a budget for the year based on the received
pledges for that year. This budget shall be approved
by the Branch at its general meeting in November.

Section 4:   Of the total amount of the budget, it is suggested
that one half shall apply to work outside the parish and the remainder to work within the parish.
(Parish is defined as local programs of local con-
gregations) The pledge to the Diocesan Episcopal
Churchwomen shall be included in the amount allotted
to work outside the parish

Section 5   The United Thank Offering and special offerings shall
be in addition to the budget.

Section 6.   Disposition of surplus funds shall be passed upon by
the Executive Board and recommended to the Branch for
approval.

Section 7   For fund-raising events, the President shall appoint
a Ways and Means Committee, consisting of the Treasurer and Secretary of Christian Social Ministries,
and at least three other members of the E C.W.

Section 8   The Ways and Means Committee, in consultation with the
Rector, shall recommend disbursements of any monies
from fund raising events. The above shall be approved
by the Executive Board before presentation to the membership.

Section 9:   The Board shall send a contribution annually to St.
Hilda's Altar Guild in memory of members who have
died during the previous year.

Section 10. Disbursement funds, listed in the budget for each officer, may be spent according to her individual judgment

Article VII
PARLIAMENTARY PROCEDURES

Section 1.   The President shall appoint a parliamentarian. _Roberts'_
Rules of Order shall be the authority for all questions
of parliamentary procedure not covered by the Constitution or By-Laws.

Section 2   The Constitution and By-Laws shall be published annually
in the Branch Yearbook

Section 3.   The Constitution and By-Laws shall be read and discussed
at the Joint Executive Board meeting in May.

Section 4   These By-Laws may be either altered or amended by a
majority of members present at any Branch meeting provided the proposed alterations have been presented to
a general meeting one month prior to the date of voting.

Section 5   All motions at Branch meetings other than those pertaining to the Constitution or By-Laws shall be decided by
a majority vote of those present

ECW Calendar 1985-86, Chapel of the Cross

August 26	Board Meeting 9:30 a.m.
September 9	General Meeting 11:30 a.m.-1:30 p.m.
September 16	Board Meeting 9:30 a.m.
October 7	General Meeting 11:30 a.m.-3:00 p.m.
October 21	Board Meeting 9:30 a.m.
November 4	General Meeting 7:30-9:00 p.m.
November 18	Board Meeting 9:30 a.m.
December 4	Quiet Day 10:30 a.m.-2:00 p.m.
January 5	Twelfth Night Party 7:00 p.m.
January 13	Board Meeting 9:30 a.m.
February 3	General Meeting 10:00-11:30 a.m.
February 17	Board Meeting 9:30 a.m.
March 3	General Meeting 11:30 a.m.-1:30 p.m.
March 17	Board Meeting 9:30 a.m.

---------------------------Easter, March 30-----------------------------

April 7	General Meeting 11:30 a.m.-2:00 p.m. (ABC Sale Luncheon)
April 12	ABC Sale
April 22-23	104th Annual Meeting, Episcopal Churchwomen Diocese of North Carolina All Saints, Roanoke Rapids
May 5	General Meeting 10:00-11:30 a.m. Installation of new officers
May 19	Old-New Board Meeting 10:00 a.m.

BUDGET   July 1, 1984 through December 31, 1985*
Episcopal Churchwomen, Chapel of the Cross

Outside Branch Expenses: $1590.00

    Church Periodical Club $ 50.00
    Christmas Gifts - Missionaries   200.00
    Convocation Fund   15.00
    Churchwomen United   50.00
    United Pledge, Diocesan Churchwomen   800.00
    Penick Home, Mother's Day Offering   100.00
    Christian Social Ministries   375.00

Inside Branch Expenses: $935.00

    Christmas Gifts (via President)   100.00
    ECW Flower Memorial   35.00
    Conference Fund   250.00
    Christian Education   225.00
    Special Groups/Chapter Fund   100.00
    Contingency Fund   150.00
    College Work/Christian Ministries   75.00

Administration: $2195.00

    Auditing   75.00
    Yearbook   675.00
    Newsletter   550.00
    Babysitting   300.00
    Administrative Supplies   400.00
      (for President, Sec., Treas.,
       Guild of Christ Child, etc.,
       Promotions, CPC, Missions, UTO)
    President's Discretionary Fund   120.00
    Luncheon Expense   75.00·

    TOTAL: $4720.00

    Note: The Child Care Scholarship Fund will receive all proceeds from the
          Hand-Me-Down Shop.

The budget reflected here was approved by the general membership at its
September 10, 1984 meeting. It covers an 18-month period. The 1986 budget
will be voted on at the November general meeting and will be published in the
ECW Newsletter.

14

EPISCOPAL CHURCHWOMEN
HISTORY

In 1881 Bishop Lyman of North Carolina asked Mrs. John Wilkes of Charlotte to start a state branch of the ten-year-old National Woman's Auxiliary to the (all-male) Board of Mission. Eleven parishes answered Mrs. Wilkes's call, and in 1882 the first meeting of the new Woman's Auxiliary was held in Tarboro. The purpose was "to do foreign and domestic mission work by means of money and goods."

The Bishop was nominally head of the organization and presided at the meetings. Each rector was defacto president of the branch, appointed all officers, and presided over the meetings. An 1892 Board of Missions report stated that a change from "auxiliary" to independence would "involve the loss of beauty, grace, and strength." The very need to make this statement suggests that some of the strong, graceful, and beautiful were chafing under male domination! Only one annual report of the women's organization is missing: 1893. Could it have included unladylike reactions to the men's 1982 report!

In 25 years the original eleven branches had grown to 123. From only making up "missionary boxes", the women's money now supported a missionary to the Philippines. Years of war and depression led to a new spirituality in the Auxiliary, and the women's obligation began to include prayer and study as well as gifts and works.

In 1958 we became the Episcopal Churchwomen of the Diocese of North Carolina, not merely "auxiliary" to the Churchmen. The women themselves, in a 1913 convention vote, had indicated the majority were not in favor of voting at parish meetings; so, when we read that in 1920, "at the suggestion of Bishop Cheshire, the women began to elect their own officers and conduct their own meetings," we have to realize the Bishop may actually have been pushing the women toward growth. In 1937 women could finally vote in parish meetings. In 1964 the proposal was made that women should be able to serve on diocesan boards, on vestries, and as delegates to Diocesan Convention. It took North Carolina men three years to give their permission.

Just as women were receiving theoretical if not always actual equal status in the church, a paradoxical threat arose. There was a churchwide movement towards integrating the work of the women with the men's and doing away with the Churchwomen as an organization. Again it is logical in theory that a group of Christians working toward common goals need not be organized by sex. In actuality, which sex would control such an integrated group and would this group push for the rights of women and children?

The Churchwomen survived. By 1973 old branches had been reorganized, new ones formed, the diocesan budget was growing, the special gifts were increasing. Browns Summit Conference Center is the result of a 1976 proposal by the women to the Bishop that they fund a study and survey for such a center.

At the 1977 General Convention the priesthood and episcopacy were opened to women. In Hebrews 11:13 the writer (thought by some scholars to be Priscilla, a New Testament Churchwoman) says "they were not yet in possession of the things promised but had seen them far ahead and hailed them." Did any of those women meeting in 1882 dare such prophecy!

Source: Jaquelin Drane Nash, *The First Hundred Years 1882-1982*

15

Chapel of the Cross
Parish Directory

1985-86

DIRECTORY OF PARISHIONERS

OCTOBER 1, 1985

- A -

Absher, Pam, E-4 Village Green Condominiums...967-1260
Adams, Anne C., 800 Woodland Ave...929-8322
Adams, Cynthia A., 508 N. Greensboro St., Carrboro 27510.........................933-0092
Adams, David J. & Maureen, 1700 Ferrell Rd.(Jonathan, Brian).....................967-5536
Adams, Edward & Polly, PO Box 2001, Southern Pines 28387.........................692-9598
Adams, Katherine, 116 Walters Rd., Carrboro 27510...............................967-1713
Aitken, Mary, 308 Briarbridge Valley Rd...929-7833
Akins, David L., & Claudia W. Frierson, 1110 Arnette Ave., Durham 27704..........
Alberti, Elizabeth & Chris, 1414 Auburndale Dr., Durham 27713..................544-2479
Alexander, Miriam H., 139 Essex Dr..
Alexander, Macy & Linn, 413 1/2 Pritchard Ave...................................929-8136
Alexander, Syd & Laurie, 510 Monroe St.(Sandy, Caroline, Laura Cole)............942-7546
Allan, Anna Brooke (Brookie), 208 Cottage Ln....................................942-1068
Allen, Dennis, Rt. 2, Box 213-B, Wake Forest 27587.............................556-6409
Allen, Dorothy, 5 Lark Circle..967-6381
Alton, Kim, $65 Fidelity Ct. Apts., 400 Davie Rd., Carrboro 27510..............942-6618
Andersen, Bob & Mary, 618 Beech Tree Ct.(Beth, Will).............................942-5655
Anderson, Allan & Lucia, 407-D McCauley St.....................................968-1321
Anderson, Charles, & Nancy Lynn Easterling, Rt. 3, Box 196, Apex 27502..........
Anderson, Joan D., 2117 Old Oxford Rd.(Jay)....................................942-1011
Anderson, Molly, 640 Craige, UNC-CH..933-3552
Anderson, Bill, Jr., 109 Quince Ln, Charlottesville, VA 22901...............804/971-7931
Andrews, Richard (Pete) & Hannah, 298 Azalea Dr.(Sarah, Chris).................929-2988
Andrews, Roberta C. (Robin), Bolin Brook Farm, Rt. 4, Box 245.................929-4884
Angyal, Andrew & Jennifer, Rt. 3, Box 578, Graham 27253 (Jeffrey, Evan).........578-2387
Applegate, Rachel Ann, 506 Craige, UNC-CH......................................933-7141
Arab, Donna, Rt. 12, Box 79..929-4699
Armitage, Edith, 2610 Stuart Dr., Durham 27707.................................489-0469
Armitage, Christopher M. & Kate, 2610 Stuart Dr., Durham 27707.(Mark, John).....489-0469
Armstrong, Ross & Carol, 424 Chateau Apts., Carrboro 27510.....................
Arnold, Thomas (Jeff) & Louise, 6001 Raleigh Dr., Tyler, TX 75703...........214-581-7877
Arnold, John F., Jr. (Jack), 8-H Post Oak Rd., Durham 27705.(John)..............383-7280
Arrowood, James & Barbara, 136 Kingston Dr.(Garrett, Heather)...................929-3408
Asby, Todd, 216 Brandan Choice, Cary 27511....................................469-1194
Askren, Carter, 3600 Tremont Dr., Apt. F-10, Durham 27705......................383-4753
Atkinson, Edward (Ned) & Laura, Fearrington Post #35, Pittsboro 27312.(Meg,Jamie)929-7660
Atwell, Alan G., Jr., 1323 Granville West.......................................933-2476
Atwill, Bill & Karen, Rt. 7, Box 251-J...968-0467
Austell, David & Amanda, 116 Walters Rd., Carrboro 27510.......................967-6573
Aycock, Denise, Rt. 2, Box 104, Warrenton 27589................................
Aydlett, Lydia, 401 Gary Rd., Carrboro 27510...................................929-7362
Ayres, Charles & Helen, 407 Knob Ct. (Jennifer, Michael).......................967-6571

Blaine, J.C.D. & Eva, 917 Greenwood Rd...942-2900
Blanchard, David, 612 Craige, UNC-CH..933-7105
Blankenship, Margaret, 103 Carol Woods...942-2645
Blocksidge, F.C. & Pearl, 13 Flemington Rd..942-1675
Blocksidge, F.C., Jr. & Martha, 328 Barclay Rd....................................929-2376
Bloom, Tom, PO Box 1026...942-4494
Blumenauer, Bill and Laney, Rt. 7, 8 Continental Trailer Park.....................967-9623
Bolick, Alan & Sandy, 843 Shadylawn Rd.(Kelly)....................................942-7367
Bolick, Jan Y., 103-A Weatherstone Dr...929-2878
Bond, Marjorie, 1111 Carol Woods..942-1997
Boston, Margaret, PO Box 2001, Southern Pines 28387..............................
Boswell, John, III & Marolyn, 3004 LaSalle St., 10-E Holly Hill, Durham 27705....383-4612
Boswell, John & Eva, 505 Morgan Creek Rd.(Julia)..................................929-5410
Bowes, Watson, Jr. & Christine, 211 Huntington Dr.(Sarah Kopplin, Rachel, Joshua
    Lucy)..929-3323
Bowman, Waldo & Virginia, 1313 Carol Woods..942-5088
Boyd, Michael, 2 Maple Dr...929-5966
Boyle, Walt, Jr., 15 Bluff Tr...967-4004
Branch, Waverly & Mary Frances, 503 Laurel Hill Rd................................942-2226
Brandes, Paul & Melba, 402 Morgan Creek Rd..929-1795
Bravo, Jose, 108 Dickerson Ct...967-5544
Braxton, Jimmy, C-12 Sharon Heights Apts..929-9191
Bray, Marsha, 717 Williams Circle...967-5626
Brescia, Christina, 3741 Bentley Dr., Durham 27707...............................489-8067
Brickley, Jack & Caroline, PO Box 1207, Pittsboro 27312..........................542-5494
Brinton, Hugh & Lillian, 12 Davie Circle..942-6750
Broadfoot, Cornelia, 2001 S. Lakeshore Dr...942-2726
Broe, Helen, PO Box 2001, Southern Pines 28387...................................
Brogden, Virginia, 1500 Duke Univ. Rd., D-3-C, Durham 27701......................489-4978
Brook, David, 2223 Creston Rd., Raleigh 27608....................................828-7121
Broughton, Annie Lee, 1111 Roosevelt Dr...942-3836
Brower, David & Lou Ann, 612 Shadylawn Rd.(Timothy, David,II, Ann)................967-4448
Brown, Charles, G-2 Univ. Garden Apts...
Brown, Mary Ann, PO Box 2035, 27515...967-7715
Brown, Mary, 121 Kenan St...942-4829
Browne, Katherine, 604 Laurel Hill Rd.(Cricket, Andrew)...........................967-4620
Brownlee, Mr. & Mrs. Richard, Jr., 239-D Jackson Circle...........................933-6743
Bruninghaus, Heidi, 132 Ridge Tr.(Marcus, Stephanie).............................967-8041
Bryan, Andrew & Judy, 103 Overland Passage..968-1081
Bryan, James (Jay), 301 Oak Ave., Carrboro 27510.(Taylor, Amanda)................929-6482
Bryan, Patricia, 1905 Overland Dr...942-0485
Bryan, Robert, Jr.(Bob), 16 Davie Circle..942-2793
Bryan, Thomas & Jani, 137 Brookberry Circle.......................................942-4365
Buchheister, Carl & Harriet, 150 Carol Woods......................................967-3409
Buck, Mary Ann, 421 Westwood Dr.(Meg)...929-2706
Buckley, Earle & Joyce, 115 Northwood Dr.(Peter & Gillian Willcox-Jones)..........942-2374
Buford, Elizabeth (Betsy), 321 E. Lane St., Raleigh 27601........................829-1204
Bullock, Marshall, PO Box 808...967-6986
Burgess, Mary, 414 Morgan Creek Rd..942-4784
Burke, Paul & Amelia (Aimee), 120 Dixie Dr.(Ann).................................967-0772
Burritt, Chuck, 109 Stephens St...942-3267
Buxton, Bill & Cathy, 2424 Sedgefield Rd. (Amy, Jake, Megan)......................942-3518
Buzby, Robin, 210 Pinegate Circle, Apt. 4...489-9488
Byerly, Wesley, III, & Marian, 103-K Westview Dr., Carrboro 27510................942-7836

Caldwell, Edward (Ted) & Katrina, 303 Plum Ln......................................929-2575
Calhoun, Carolyn, 5-E Towne House Apts...929-8779
Callan, Anne, 2729 Circle Dr., Durham 27705.......................................
Calver, Mr. & Mrs. Robert B., 133 Berry Patch.....................................967-5811
Calverly, Eliza, Carol Woods Health Center..
Cameron, Edward & Emily, 404 Laurel Hill Rd.......................................942-4742
Cameron, Molly, 1 Lanark Rd...967-7498
Campbell, David & Marcia, 162 Ridge Tr.(John, Chapin).............................942-8265
Campbell, Tacy, Carol Woods Health Center, D-60...................................929-4619
Campbell, Karen, 3545 Mayfair St., #202, Durham 27707.............................493-0836
Campbell, William & Sabra, 1015 Roosevelt Dr.(Brent).............................967-5096
Cantrell, Mark, 314 Coachway..967-9909
Capettini, Robert (Bob) & Jane, 17887 Creciente Way, San Diego, CA 92127 (Allison,Challen)
Capowski, Carolyn, 408 Coolidge St.(Byron Clayton)...............................929-1670
Carmichael, Ann, Tower Manager, Granville East...................................933-0502
Carpenter, Rebecca, 9-I Estes Park Apts., Carrboro 27510.........................929-8192
Carr, Fred & Anna, 900 E. Franklin St.(Joshua, Jacob)...........................967-0354
Carter, Anna, 3 Village Mobile Home Pk...967-0088
Carter, Anne: see SCHUNIOR, Charles
Carter, Anne S., 108 Juniper Ct., Spartanburg, SC 29302..........................
Carter, Mary, C-8 Estes Park Apts., Carrboro 27510...............................942-2563
Cartwright, James, Jr. & Laurie, 310 Umstead Dr.(Donna, Breck, Philip)...........929-7998
Carver, Theresa, 105 Ridgewood Pk, Rt. 5...967-6067
Case, Harry & Elinor, 188 Carol Woods..967-4194
Castle, Beth B., A-16 Woodbridge Apts., Carrboro 27510...........................
Catanzaro, Christine de: see DE CATANZARO, Christine
Cates, Anne, 329 Tenney Circle...942-2161
Cathers, Dorothy, 250 S. Estes Dr., #42...929-3289
Cauthen, Kenneth: see FISH, Gloria
Cavalaris, Chris, 109 Hillsborough St..968-1089
Caywood, Kathryn: see ROBERTSON, Philmore
Cecil-Fronsman, Bill, & Sally Fronsman-Cecil, Rt. 4, Pineview Estates #21 (Thea).929-1926
Chacko, Tom, 206 McCauley St..967-2521
Chamberlain, Emily, 2449 Mayberry Ct...967-4417
Chambers, David R., 315 N. Boundary St., Apt. C, Raleigh 27602...................755-1559
Chambers, Michael & Carol, 1412 Valley Run, Durham 27707.(Amanda)................489-8714
Champion, Margaret, 1819 N. Lakeshore Dr.(Bobby, Johnny, Beth Anne)..............967-5820
Chandler, William & Catherine, 523 E. Rosemary St................................942-5547
Chaney, Lillian, 1821 N. Lakeshore Dr.(Larrette, Bethany, Edward)................929-1719
Chaney, Larrette, PO Box 8664, College Station, Williamsburg, VA 23186...........
Chapman, Beth, 519 E. Jones St., Raleigh 27601...................................
Chapman, Margaret, Rt. 9, Box 505..929-4823
Charlton, John & Lynn, Rt. 2, Box 729.(Laura)...................................929-9202
Cheape, Kathleen (Kitty), 9 Cobb Terrace...942-1922
Cherry, Robert, C-38 Carol Woods Health Center...................................
Chris, James & Linda, 8 Sutton Pl.(Melissa, Nicole)..............................929-7834
Church, Carl, & Carol Holtzclaw, Rt. 1, Box 4, Blueberry Hill, Pittsboro 27312...929-2014
Churchill, Larry & Sande, 406 Overland Dr.(Shelley, Blair).......................967-6955
Claris, C. David, 112 S. Peak St., Carrboro 27510................................967-1782
Clark, Henry & Blanche, 1425 Gray Bluff Tr.......................................933-7007
Clark, Victoria, 5-F Royal Park Apts., Carrboro 27510............................933-5093
Clarke, Molly, Hillhaven Convalescent Center, 1602 E. Franklin St................967-2911

Crowther, Hal, & Lee Smith, 44 Cedar St...968-3808
Cryer, Barbara. 711 Greenwood Rd..967-7886
Culpepper, Lee, 620 Park Pl...967-6782
Curtis, Margaret (Peggy), B-8 Colony Apts...933-9453
Cuttino, John & Grace (Jace),20 Wysteria Way.(Jay, Joy, David)....................929-5186

- D -

Daisley, Mike, 333-R Circle Ave., Charlotte 28207............................704/334-2135
Dale, William (Bill) & Jane, 813 Churchill Dr.....................................929-6180
Dallmeyer, Dottie, 711 Emory Dr.(Rudi, Anne, Lisha, Dirk).........................967-6819
Daniel, Anne, #6 Vauxhall Pl..493-7078
Daniel, Sophie, P.O. Box 734..933-6049
Daniel, Walter & Elizabeth, 2109 Sunset Ave., Durham 27705.......................
Daniell, William & Marcia, 908 Coker Dr...929-3843
Dansby, Surada, 127 North St.(Taylor)...968-1144
Darley, Kathleen, 1205 Carol Woods..929-5149
Dauchert, Eugene & Katherine, 3 Pine Tree Ln.(Jonathan, Stephen)..................493-4130
Daugherty, Rich & Phyllis, 4706 Berini Dr., Durham 27705.........................383-6770
Davidson, Edna, 214 Hillcrest Circle..942-6564
Davidson, Jonathan & Meg, 637 Totten Pl.(Ben, Becky)..............................942-2933
Davis, Addison & Kathryn, 409 Brandywine.(Carolyn & Christopher Baumgardner)......942-0604
Davis, Bob & Trisha, 132 Hunter's Ridge Rd.(Kristy, Ginger).......................929-6536
Davis, Gordon & Joan, 1200 LeClair St...929-6377
Davis, Helen, 2709 Sarah Ave., Durham 27707......................................
Davis, James & Frances, 405 Westwood Dr...942-3661
Davis, Lois, 155 Carol Woods..968-8009
Davis, Ron & Lucy, 705 Gimghoul Rd.(Ron, Margaret, Lisbeth).......................929-5218
Davis, Ronald Redd, 1001 Raleigh Rd...942-1999
Davis, Steve & Brenda, 308 Rainbow Dr., Carrboro 27510 (Laura)...................942-0467
Dawkins, Mary, 100 Aberdeen Ct., Carrboro 27510.(Marantha, Caleb)................942-3362
Dawson, Alice, 304 Glendale Dr..967-1640
Dawson, Al & Deborah, Chalet Apts., K., Greene St.(John Alexander)................942-7489
Dawson, Gretchen, 205 Hunterhill Rd...
Day, Dianne, 120 Northampton Terrace..942-1418
Day, James, 13-I Towne House Apts...929-3019
De Boy, Kathleen, 208-A Hillsborough Rd., Carrboro 27510.........................
Dean, Tom, The Courtyard, W. Franklin St..942-5154
Dearman, Henry (Hank) & Emily, 422 Fair Oaks Cir.(Emily).........................967-5743
Deasey, Mary: see COLLINS, Brad
Deaver, Elizabeth: see ALBERTI, Elizabeth
de Catanzaro, Christine, 110-B Estes Dr., Carrboro 27510.........................929-4837
DeGraff, Sally, Rt. 1, Box 201-2, Durham 27705.(Jonah Winterhalder)..............942-1478
deLuca, Emilie, 614 E. Franklin St..942-3724
Dennis, Lillian, 119 Fidelity Ct., A-1, Carrboro 27510...........................
DeSaix, Peter & Jean, 327 Forbush Mountain Dr.(Amy, Anna)........................929-1580
Detweiler, George & Simone, 15 Matchwood, Fearrington Post, Pittsboro 27312......933-9652
Devine, John & Janet, 311 Old Forest Creek Dr.(Molly, Jean)......................929-2424
DeVoe, Hazel, 182 Carol Woods...967-4305
DeWinter, Walter J. (Bud), 105 Keith Rd., Carrboro 27510.........................929-5441
Dey, K.V. & Pat, Rt. 5, 108 Fox Run...967-8558
Dickerman, Carol, 504-D N. Greensboro St., Carrboro 27510 (Beth)................929-0765

D-6

Dickerman, James (Jim), 103 Longwood Dr.(Beth)...................................493-5059
Dickerson, Deanna, c/o Halifax Community College, PO Drawer 809, Weldon, NC 27890.537-8762
Diffey, John & Martha, 514 North St.(Matthew)....................................933-8772
Dill, David & Martha, 917 Emory Dr.(Matthew, Caitlin)............................967-4758
Dixon, John & Vivian, 216 Glenhill Ln..929-1020
Dixon, William & Carol, Rt. 5, Box 226-B.(Jessie)................................942-6986
Doak, George & Pokie, P.O. Box 853..942-4576
Dobbs, Jo, 2216 Payne St., Evanston, IL 60201...................................
Doepner, Tripp, 102-B Todd St., Carrboro 27510..................................
Dominguez, Francisco (Frank) & Patricia, 1439 Poinsett Dr.(Katie, Charles).......933-5020
Douglass, E.P., 711 Bradley Rd...929-5653
Douglass, Fenner & Jane, 37 Pearce-Mitchell, Stanford, CA 94305..................
Drake, David & Victoria, PO Box 4709, Duke Sta., Durham 27706...................
'Ducey, Mitchell, & Donna Metcalfe, 87-A Weaver Dairy Rd.........................942-8500
Dudley, Ken, 5311 Pelham Rd., Durham 27707......................................544-2461
Dugan, Nancy, 1207 Carol Woods..942-5364
Duke, Kenneth, 3600 Tremont Dr., Apt. F-10, Durham 27702........................383-4753
Dula, James, III & Jennifer, 77 Tar Heel Mobile Ct..............................967-9308
Durham, Eddie & Dockery, Rt. 1, Box 354, Wildcat Creek Rd.(Carrie, Ced)..........967-3370
Durrill, Wayne K., 753 Old Mill Rd..929-2005
Dyer, Jane, 4007 Cornwallis Rd., Durham 27705.(Leroy Van Veld)...................489-8206
Dykes, Frances, PO Box 865..942-2706
Dzierlenga, Stan & Jackie, 105 Bristol Dr. (Scott, Casey).......................967-5195

- E. -

Earle, Carole, 436 Northside Dr.(Mike, Jeff, Kevin).............................942-1008
Easterling, Nancy Lynn: see ANDERSON, Charles
Eckblad, John & Martine, 637 Kensington Dr.(Ben, Josh, Marie)...................968-4740
Eckfeldt, Anne, 10-C Stratford Hills Apts.......................................942-2465
Edkins, Marie, PO Box 2001, Southern Pines 28387................................
Edsall, Mary W., 204 Bruton Dr.(Elizabeth, Robert)..............................967-0711
Egan, Bruce & Chris, 250 S. Estes Dr., #115 (Emily, John).......................929-1485
Egan, Wesley & Ruth, 1303 Mason Farm Rd...929-1886
Egan, Wesley, Jr. (Wes), & Virginia, 1303 Mason Farm Rd.........................929-1886
Elder, Francis (Frank) & Virginia, 151 Carol Woods..............................942-1544
Elkins-Williams, Steve & Betsy, 406 Knob Ct.(Tyler & Peter).....................967-9569
Ellett, R. Scott, Rt. 12, Box 4...929-6089
Ellington, Richard & Alice, 109 Bruton Dr.(Elizabeth Claire)....................967-4168
Emerson, Everett & Katherine, 130 Lake Ellen Dr.................................967-2652
Emmel, Tom & Barbara, 106 Braswell Ct.(Sarah)...................................942-3141
Engel, Frauke E., 116-B Purefoy Rd..929-7138
English, Ellen M., 2920 Chapel Hill Rd., #2-A, Durham 27707.....................493-2007
Englund, Jamie, 205-A Hunterhill Rd...
Ensign, Marty, 1214 Carol Woods...967-0019
Epple, William & Jeanne, PO Box 3012, 27515.....................................929-9113
Epps, Garrett & Spencer Love, 902 Roosevelt Dr., #4.(Daniel)....................929-5215
Ericksen, Jim & Helen, 14 Hilltop MHP...968-0230
Erskine, Christine G.: see PHILLIPS, Robert
Erwin, Billie, 107 Jones St..942-4574
Esser, George & Mary, 211 Elliott Rd..929-9297
Eubanks, Mr. & Mrs. David, 706 Williams Circle..................................
Eudy, David & Julie, 99 Brier Patch Lane..929-9053

D-7

Evans, Arthur & Iris, 11 Banbury Ln..
Evans, Virginia, 219 E. Franklin St..967-9176
Ewell, H.J. & Toni, 205 Marilyn Ln...

- F -

Faherty, Victoria (Tori), 410 Brookside Dr...
Fahrer, Richard (Rick) & Miriam, 109 Hudson Hills, Pittsboro 27312.(Adrian)......542-2557
Farris, Gary & Elizabeth, PO Box 3671, 27515,.(Jason, Arkeketah, Chadonayhe)......542-3545
Fenhagen, F. Weston & Betsy Y., 409 Lakeshore Ln.....................................933-5760
Ferguson, Frances, 509 Dogwood Dr..929-4865
Ferguson, Bruce & Candice, 3201 Hornbuckle Pl., Durham 27707....................688-1407
Ferrell, Bonnie, 1208 Ellen Pl.(Kelly Ann, Brian)...................................933-2022
Ferrell, Joseph, 2 Buttons Rd..967-3932
Farrell, Tenley F., 322 James, UNC-CH..
Fickel, Louise, 909-A Dawes St...929-6980
Fickes, Gudrun F., 0-13 Colony Apts..942-1850
Fields, Henry & Anne, 1912 White Plains Rd.(Ben, Justin).............................967-5573
Fillipo, Drew, 120-C Cheek Ave., Carrboro 27510.....................................
Finch, Mathilde, 75 Maxwell Rd...929-4490
Finks, Lee, 363 Wesley Dr.(Wilson, Catherine, Charlie)...............................967-7254
Finney, Frances, 845 Shadylawn Rd..929-7587
Finson, Jon, 203-A Justice St..942-5046
Fischbeck, Lisa: see MILLER, Charles
Fish, Gloria H., & Kenneth Cauthen, 102 Lindsay St., Carrboro 27510.............942-8717
Fish, Steve, V-8 Old Well Apts., Carrboro 27510.....................................968-8143
Fisher, Page & Joyce, 1 Stoneridge Cir., Durham 27707...............................493-1218
Fisher, James & Evelyn, 412 Tinkerbell Rd.(Evelyn, Dede).............................967-1479
Fisher, Mark & Ele, 400 Bowling Creek Rd...929-9172
Fleming, Anne, 108 Garden St...967-3263
Fletcher, Frances, PO Box 925..929-1035
Floyd, Connie, 5-B Royal Park Apts., Carrboro 27510.................................933-3086
Floyd, Josephine, 175 Hamilton Rd..967-7388
Fogle, Richard & Catherine, 511 E. Rosemary St.......................................929-5602
Folds, James & Carolyn, 635 Arlington St.(James, Jr., David)..........................929-7423
Foley, Leslie A., 8-A Post Oak Rd., Durham 27705....................................
Ford, Mary Anne, 403 Elliott Rd..933-5404
Forsyth, John & Diane, 831 Kenmore Rd.(David, Dayna).................................967-4040
Forsythe, Barney & Jane, 150-C Lee Rd., West Point, NY 10996.(Jennifer, Bryant)..
Fort, Lucy, 36-8 S. Circle Dr..942-3606
Fortney, David, PO Box 772...967-3099
Foster, Judy, 211 Henderson St...967-0552
Fountain, Barbara Ann, Rt. 6, Lot 53, The Timbers MHP, Hillsborough 27278........732-9557
Fouts, James & Joan, 212 Ridge Trail.(Jeff)..929-6101
Fox, Robert, 106 Northampton Plaza...967-8411
Frampton, Paul, Fearrington Post, Box 32, Pittsboro 27312...........................933-0702
Francis, Allen & Edith, 158 Carol Woods..929-4190
Francis, Janet, 120 Ridge Trail, Village West..967-1155
Frankstone, David & Frances, 304 N. Boundary St.(Susan, Lee)........................929-0073
Frantz, Paul & Mary, 502 Sharon Rd.(Kristin Harper, Heather)........................929-7433
Frauenfelder, David, 345 Craige, UNC-CH..933-7224
Freeman, James & Elizabeth, 125 Fearrington, Pittsboro 27312.......................929-6649
Friend, Shannon, 301 Everett, UNC-CH...933-1654

Frierson, Claudia W.: see AKINS, David

Froelich, Molly, 140 Ridge Trail..929-4113

Fronsman-Cecil, Sally: see CECIL-FRONSMAN, Bill

Frost, Nancy, G-12 Village Green.(Andy, Ashley)............................933-7190

Fuller, Edmund & Ann, Fearrington Post, Box 160, Pittsboro 27312..............542-5022

Fuller, Janie, 325 W. University Dr...942-4869

- G -

Gaddy, Susan, 315 Northampton Terrace.......................................967-3577

Gales, Ginger, 129 Kingsbury Dr...967-1952

Gallimore, Mike & Stephanie, 108 Falls Dr.(David, Michael)..................383-9329

Gallis, Harry & Susie, Rt. 8, Box 37, Chesidy Circle.(Alex, Sara)...........489-8495

Gallman, Eve, Rt. 2, Box 264, Graham 27523.................................376-3066

Gann, Layne, 12-A University Lake Apts., Carrboro 27510.....................

Gantt, Courtney: see TURNER, Susan

Garceau, Lincoln, 203 Carol St., Carrboro 27510............................967-6956

Gardiner, Frances, 402 Granville Rd...942-1965

Gardner, Robert & Harolyn, 904 Grove St.(Steven, Kirsten)..................942-7622

Garner, Leslie H., Jr. & Katrina, 214 Hillsborough St.(Brantley)...........929-8918

Gaskins, Ruth, PO Box 2642, 27515..

Gass, Gretchen, 223 Northampton Terrace....................................933-9032

Gass, Mark & Cynthia, 1409 Virginia Ave., Durham 27705.....................

Gates, Charles & Marie-Henriette, 400 Mimosa Dr............................489-9457

Getz, Jackie, Rt. 7, Box 158...933-5682

Gibbs, Kathryn Lee, PO Box 516...

Gill, Douglas & Lydia, 850 E. Massachusetts Ave., Southern Pines 28387..........

Gilley, Kim, D-6 Shepherd Lane...933-5081

Gilligan, Peter, & Lynn Smiley, 102 Fox Run................................967-5893

Givens, Margaret, 2201 Carol Woods...942-6105

Glassock, Blythe, 102 Westbury Ct.(Robson).................................929-9329

Gleason, Ralph & Betty, 7 Fearrington Post, Pittsboro 27312.................942-0552

Gless, Darryl & Ruth, 208 Celeste Circle...................................493-8097

Glover, Murrell & Erma, 4 Lystra Estates, Rt. 9............................942-5936

Godfrey, James & Eleanor, 231 Hillcrest Circle.............................967-1806

Godschalk, Lallie, 209 Glendale.(David)....................................929-5013

Gold, Jennifer, 2152 Lakeshore Ct..967-7743

Goldfinch, John & Carolyn, 623 Summit St., Winston-Salem 27101.(Jay, Martha).....

Golia-Paladin, David: see SAUTER, Suzanne

Gomer, Diane, 409 Fair Oaks Circle.(Lauren)................................942-7057

Goodwin, Bonnie, 22 Batts Hill Rd., New Bern 28560.........................

Govan, Mrs. James, 420 Whitehead Circle....................................967-7670

Gowan, Ann, PO Box 9957, Duke Sta., Durham 27706...........................684-7870

Grace, Jeffrey & Risa, 2920 Chapel Hill Rd., 19-C, Durham 27707............493-6786

Graetzer, Dan, D-10 Village Green...967-2417

Graham, Margaret, 2705 Stuart Dr., Durham 27707.(Will, Cameron)............489-2020

Grandis, Arnold & Fanny, 3414 Angus Rd., Durham 27705.(Eppie, Amy, Stephen)....489-2685

Gravely, Susan, 25 Bluff Tr..

Gray, Peg, Rt. 9, Box 425-G..933-3839

Green, Bobbe, 602 Emory Dr...933-2037

Green, Patricia M., 54-B Davie Circle......................................933-8401

Greene, John & Katherine, 107 Carl Dr., Rt. 4.(Michael, Katie).............967-4063

Greenhill, Jim, 321 W. Cameron Ave...968-9062

```
Greenlund, Terry, PO Box 331.........................................................967-4387
Greer, Joe & Sarah, The Meadows, 21 Clover Dr........................................942-8232
Greer, Thomas (Trey) & Joanne, 29 Cedar Ct., Carrboro 27510..........................967-1169
Gregg, Robert (Bob) & Mary Layne, 218 Vance St.(Clark, Andrew, Courtney, Amy).....967-4114
Greulach, Elizabeth (Libby), 1815 S. Lakeshore Dr....................................942-6558
Grey, Richard & Elizabeth, 306 Estes Dr. Ext., Apt. B-1, Carrboro 27510.........929-8439
Griffin, Sandra S., Rt. 11, Riffel Woods 6...........................................929-4360
Griggs, Eugene S., F-7 Camelot Village...............................................968-8616
Griggs, Patty, 8 Cobb Terrace........................................................929-6829
Gronde, Jeffrey, 6 Rocky Knoll Apts..................................................929-6299
Groo, Virginia L., 112-B Purefoy Rd..................................................967-8645
Grubbs, Marilyn: see HARDY, Albert
Guild, Doug & Connie, 124 Murdock Rd., Hillsborough 27278............................732-7306
Gunnels, John & Lavan, Rt. 7, Box 653-D..............................................942-8640
Gunselman, Dan & Elizabeth, 1708 Wallace St., Durham 27707.(Lawrence, Patrick)...544-7235
Gunter, Harvey, 208 Whitfield Rd., Rt. 7, Durham 27707...............................489-4674
Gurkin, Katherine (Kitty), 106 Polks Tr..............................................942-1280
Gustafson, Thomas (Gus) & Cathy, 1 Little Spring Ln., Durham 27707
    (Eric, Thomas, Craig, Daniel)....................................................493-3920


                                    - H -


Habel, David & Barbara, 306 Briar Bridge Valley......................................933-8109
Hackney, Betsy, 104 Carolina Forest.(Daniel).........................................967-3822
Hackney, Charles (Chuck), A-2 Village Green...........................................942-7786
Haebig, Jon & Mimi, 103 Highland Dr.(Paul, Ann, Steve)...............................967-6169
Hagood, Jimmy, 234 McCauley St.......................................................942-3679
Hails, Linda, 3122 Dixon Rd., Durham 27707...........................................489-8809
Hairston, Nelson & Martha (Patty), 1008 Highland Woods...............................929-9456
Hales, Kenneth, PO Box 3213, 27515...................................................929-0100
Hall, Ginger, Rt. 4, Box 1057, Hillsborough 27278....................................732-5635
Hall, Julie, 704 N. Columbia St......................................................929-1463
Hall, Louise, 305 Granville Rd.......................................................942-1625
Hall, Sarah, PO Box 2001, Southern Pines 28387.......................................
Hall, Timothy & Helen, 303 Country Club Rd.(Hilary & Lucas Root).....................967-9739
Hamilton, Carol, 517 E. Franklin St..................................................967-2561
Hammond, John & Mary, 108 Hunter Hill Rd.(Stephen)...................................929-0074
Hampson, Neil & Diane, 3224-B Myra St., Durham 27707.(Lindsay).......................493-4386
Hancock, Frank, 419 Tinkerbell Rd....................................................
Haney, James & Louise, 719 Braniff Dr., Cary, NC 27511...............................
Hanger, Mr. & Mrs. Herbert, 16 Lanier Dr.............................................933-0070
Harbin, Leisa, 0-8 Kingswood Apts....................................................968-1087
Hardaker, William & Roberta, 2702 Spencer St., Durham 27705.(Tracy, Ryan, Wllm.).489-1965
Hardison, Thomas, 205 Butternut Dr...................................................929-8793
Hardy, Albert, & Marilyn Grubbs, Rt. 1, Box 201-6, Durham 27705.(Joseph)........942-7193
Hargrove, Albert (Al), PO Box 1141...................................................967-6778
Harkness, Jean, 12-F Sharon Heights Apts.............................................942-7631
Harper, Kevin, 410 Melanie Ct........................................................929-1581
Harrington, Leslie, 832 Shadylawn Rd.(Timothy).......................................929-8218
Harris, Tyndall & Mary, PO Box 2533..................................................489-7371
Harris, Tyndall, Jr. & Cyndi, Rt. 1, Box 152, Pittsboro 27312.(Tyndall, III).....942-5678
Harrison, Katherine (Kitty), 404 Mimosa Dr...........................................493-3781
Harrison, Nathalie, 605 Shady Lawn Rd................................................929-2457
```

Harrison, Melody: see POPIO, Ken
Harrison, William M. (Bo), 303 F. Franklin St.....................................968-1083
Harriss, Tom, PO Box 3321, 27515..
Hart, Larry & Martha, 800 Churchill Dr...929-0081
Hart, Thomas V., 213 Swain Hall, 044-A, UNC-CH....................................
Hart, Todd, 321 W. Cameron Ave...968-9062
Hartogensis, Laura, 1118 Carol Woods...942-7826
Hartzo, Dorothea H., 1208 Carol Woods..942-1686
Harve, Karen, 522 Craige, UNC-CH...933-3585
Harvey, Hugh & Lois, 11 Elmstead Pl..544-5001
Hausler, Shelley, Rt. 7, Box 656-C.(Maura, Kurt, Mark)...........................933-5467
Hawkins, Alec, 1508 Granville West...933-2541
Hawley, Susan, 406 Clayton Rd..929-3738
Hayes, Betsy, 305 W. University Dr.(Cinc, Creighton).............................929-5907
Hayes, Charles, Rt. 1, Box 341-B, Snow Camp 27349...............................
Hayes, Paul & Roxanne, 12 Lanark Rd..968-4414
Hazlett, Mary Elizabeth (Ibby), 3114 Carol Woods.................................942-3585
Healy, Jim, PO Box 778, Hillsborough 27278.(Laura, Mary)........................942-1536
Heffner, Tom & Kathie, 103 Porter Pl.(Gray, Hunt)...............................929-4637
Helwig, Janet, G-6 The Villages, Carrboro 27510.................................967-7532
Henderson, William (Will), 1307 Carol Woods......................................929-2466
Henson, John R., 221 Nature Tr...933-6925
Herbert, Bill & Marsha, 243 Hillcrest Circle.(Turner, Coleman)...................929-8905
Herman, Nick & Suzanne, 103 Woodbridge Ln.(Allison)..............................
Hernandez, Jeanne, 433 Brookside.(John, Peter)...................................942-6560
Hesla, Ann, 114 Walden Dr.(Britta, Molly)..942-2705
Hesla, Timothy, c/o Institute of Nutrition, 311 Pittsboro St.....................966-1094
Hewitt, Laura, 321 Winston, UNC-CH...933-6232
Hexter, Jon, 2505 Granville South..933-5657
Hicks, James & Laurinda, 109 Turnage Rd.(Vivian, Rebecca, James).................967-5628
Hickson, Francis V., 106 W. Carr St., #1, Carrboro 27510........................967-3908
Hiday, Lanny, 1424 Arboretum Dr..929-2631
Hierman, Donald & Carol, 114 Tradescant Dr.(Todd, Stacey)........................942-6085
Higgins, Thomas & Eva, 708 Wellington Dr.(Amy, Taylor)..........................929-5422
High, David & Alvis, 5211 Pelham Rd., Durham 27713.............................544-2602
Highriter, Mildred, 2106 Carol Woods...929-1915
Highriter, Marion, 311 Oakland Ln..929-4273
Hileman, Barbara, 101-B Todd St., Carrboro 27510................................967-0185
Hill, Carolyn, Wesleyan Academy, PO Box 1489, Guaynabo, PR 00657................
Hill, Watts & Anne, 1001 Raleigh Rd..
Hilton, Kathy, 1715 Curtis Rd..967-4587
Hinson, Billy R., Jr. & Jane, 2829 Split Rail Pl., Durham 27702.................383-6782
Hoard, Steve, 128 Ridge Trail..
Hoare, Geoffrey, 4109-A Cross Creek Ct., Raleigh 27607..........................781-8623
Hobgood, Ann, 250 S. Estes Dr., #81.(Ted, Buffy)................................929-9623
Hodges, Stacey, 13-C Towne House Apts..933-1798
Hodges-Copple, John & Anne, 2321 Honeysuckle Rd..................................933-9129
Hodgson, Robert E., PO Box 84, Bynum 27228......................................942-7682
Hoerning, Thomas E., 218 Ehringhaus, UNC-CH......................................
Hoggard, Norfleet, C-2 Oak Terrace Apts..967-2379
Hollis, Gary & Melonie, O-8 Royal Park Apts., Carrboro 27510....................933-9241
Holmesley, Fariba Golkho, 4-A Oak Terrace Apts...................................929-6491
Holshauser, Laura, 802 The Oaks..968-0083
Holt, Merrill & Cynthia, PO Box 3097, 27515......................................933-9729
Holtzclaw, Carol: see CHURCH, Carl

- I -

- J -

Jackson, Amy, 5102 Chapel Hill Blvd., Durham 27707...............................
Jackson, Martha, 209 Conner Dr., Apt. 14.............................942-4703
Jackson, Mathue (Matt), 141 California Ave., 306, Palo Alto, CA 94306............
Jamerson, Ann Lou, 48 Davie Circle...................................929-1346
Jamerson, Anna, 910 Roosevelt Dr.....................................942-4727
James, Michael (Mike) & Carol, PO Box 3464, 27515....................929-3380
Jaques, Paul & Non, 28 Whitley Dr.(Rhien, Jane, Benjamin)............942-5891
Jeck, Lida, 2420 Alpine Rd., Durham 27707.(William Richard)..........493-4806
Jeney, Patricia, 20-H Stratford Hills Apts...........................968-1543
Jenner, Helen, 809 Shadylawn Rd......................................942-7123
Jobson, Robert, 209 Fearrington Post, Pittsboro 27312................542-4747
Johnson, Mr. & Mrs. H.S., 105 Tanglewood Ln., Carrboro 27510.........942-0288
Johnson, Jim, 3517 Brecknock St., Durham 27705.......................493-1172
Johnson, Julie A., 106 Pinegate Circle, #11..........................489-9730
Johnson, Margaret, 104 Jones St......................................942-1527
Johnson, Norman L., 206 Short St.....................................967-7660
Johnson, Sarah, 1516 Clermont Rd., Durham 27713......................544-5080
Johnston, Paul & Janet, 113 Windsor Circle (Henry)...................929-9681
Johnston, Terrance (Terry), & Robin, Rt. 3, Box 337.(Peter, Merrimon)............933-0097
Jones, Annie Lee, 3103 Carol Woods...................................929-1665
Jones, Mabel, 804 King's Mill Rd.....................................929-2094
Jones, Claiborne, 419 Westwood Dr....................................942-2722
Jones, Connie, 39-H Laurel Ridge Apts................................968-0023
Jones, Lawrence, 102 Fraternity Ct...................................968-9136
Jordan, Kathleen, 521 Green St., Durham 27701........................683-8003
Jordan, John & Gloria, 100 Calumet Ct., Carrboro 27510.(April, Dana,John)........967-7379
Jordan, Lisa, 330 Wesley Dr..967-1875
Jordan, Lynn, 1047 James, UNC-CH.....................................933-4964
Jordan, Stacy, PO Box 5474, Duke Sta., Durham 27706..................684-7177

- K -

Kahler, Stephen & Julia (Pem), 312 Granville Rd. (Jean)..............942-3667
Kaluzny, Arnold & Barbara, 102 Pine Ln.(Melissa).....................967-5566
Keagy, Blair & Kathleen (Kathy), 2450 Sedgefield Rd.(Matthew, Kristin)...........929-6556
Keathley, Edward & Mary Ann, 520 Ashley Ct., Foxcroft Apts...........942-7642
Kelly, Barbara, 158 Ridge Tr...942-1215
Kelly, Isabelle, B-5 Colony Apts.....................................967-0486
Kent, Richard (Rick) & Betty, 102 Cedar Hills Circle.(Sheila, David).............929-6483
Kern, Fred D., 3600 Tremont Dr., C-10, Durham 27705..................383-1342
Kern, Julie, 41-B The Home Place, 200 Woodcroft, Durham 27713........489-7132
Kernan, Peter & Catherine, 407 Pritchard Ave.........................
Kessler, Eugene & Mary, 1508 Cumberland Rd...........................968-1066
Kessler, Ridley, Jr. & Diane, 200 Oleander Dr.(Melissa), Carrboro 27510..........929-1955
Kiffney, Pat, Rt. 3, Box 628, Hillsborough 27278.....................929-6009
Killebrew, Paul D., 22-H Stratford Hills Apts........................967-0617
Killeffer, Josephine, 736 E. Franklin St.............................942-4221
Killion, Steve & Laura, 105 Estes Dr. Ext., Carrboro 27510...........929-4831
King, Karen, 23 Red Pine Rd..929-8049
King, Kimball & Harriet, 610 North St.(Caleb, Virginia)..............942-4224

D-13

King, Lowell & Liz, 4101 Five Oaks Dr., #41, Durham 27707.....................489-9417
Klimkowski, Kim, 201 Everett, UNC-CH...
Kling, Cindy, D-1 Colony Apts..933-7473
Knight, Gretchen, 5918 Williamsburg Way, Durham 27713............................
Knoerr, Margaret, 208 Hillsborough St...942-4095
Koch, Bruno & Patricia, 1540 Ferrell Rd.(Bruno, Theodore).......................942-6637
Koch, Harriet, 159 Hamilton Rd..967-4354
Koch, Trude: see SHAHADY< Tom
Koch, William & Dorothy (Dot), 104 Stoneybrook Rd...............................942-1351
Koelle, Virginia, 312 Ridgecrest Dr...942-6761
Kohut, Frances Speas, 2729 Bartram Rd., Winston-Salem 27106......................
Kolodny-Creech, Mary, 118 Iredell St., Durham 27705.............................286-7814
Kopp, Vincent & Katherine, 738-A Gimghoul Rd.(Margaret).........................933-8383
Kopytowski, Dan & Debbie, 2219 O'Brien St., G'boro 27407 (Danielle, Dominique)...855-3391
Kozell, Mark & Suzanne, 422 Constitution Ave., Durham 27705.....................489-6913
Krebs, Florence & Patricia, 309 Elliott Rd......................................967-7209
Kreps, Clifton & Juanita, 3511 Cambridge Rd., Durham 27705......................286-3701
Krishnamoorlty, Charu, Dept. of Statistics, Phillips Hall, UNC-CH................942-5602
Kuhl, Thorn & Mary, 603 Bolin Creek Dr., Carrboro 27510.........................967-9164
Kuralt, Mary-Catherine, 110 Walters Rd., Carrboro 27510.........................967-1716
Kuzil, Lee, 136 Tuscarora Ave., Hillsborough 27278..............................

- L -

Lackey, Miles M., PO Box 1094, Shelby 28150.....................................
Lackey, Robin, 403 Forest Ct., Carrboro 27510...................................942-6908
Lamb, Mr. & Mrs. James C., 313 Woodhaven Rd.....................................942-1310
Lamont, Louise, 300 Laurel Hill Rd..967-3488
Lamprecht, Virginia (Ginzy), 302 W. Main St., Carrboro 27510....................967-6547
Lantz, Priscilla, 16-I Sharon Heights Apts......................................968-1296
Lathrop, Tony, 250 S. Estes, #101...967-4428
Laub, Rick, Rt. 3, Box 311, Fayetteville Rd., Durham 27713......................544-6073
Law, Charles & Vickie, 1515 Bramble Dr., Durham 27712.(Blake)...................471-9161
Lawson, Edward (Ned) & Rebecca (Becki),Hohenweg #4,D-6901 Schonau ODW, W. Germany
Le, Thanh & Hoa Thu, D-6 Elliott Woods Apts.(Tam, Tuyen)........................
Lea, James & Diane, 2154 Lakeshore Ct.(Christopher, Susanna)....................967-5134
Leach, Sandy, 131-C Mason Farm Rd...967-0448
Lee, Charles & Nancy, 105 Finley Forest Dr......................................933-6359
Lee, Cornelia, 15 Dogwood Acres Dr..942-7242
Lee, Elizabeth, 3325 Mossdale Ave., Durham 27707................................
Lee, Peter & Kristy, 524 E. Franklin St.(Stewart, Jamey)........................967-6023
Lee, Sherman & Ruth, 102 Dixie Dr...968-0737
Leeper, Beth, 2200 Chapel Hill Rd., Durham 27707................................493-3757
Leete, Susan: see THOMPSON, Tommy
Lefler, Michael & Vickie, 303 The Oaks Apts.(Courtney)..........................942-0110
Leigh, Laurence & Marcella, 205 Conner Dr.......................................933-6462
Lenchek, Karen, 106 Scarlett Dr...933-5016
Lester, Memory A., 413 Fair Oaks Circle...942-6826
Leuchtenburg, Jean W., 505 Hawthorne Lane (Christopher).........................967-1257
Lewis, Alice E., Rt. 5, Box 108, Charlie Tew Ct., Hillsborough 27278............732-5728
Lewis, Hilda, 1204 Willow Dr..967-7737
Lewis, Henry, 407 North St..942-1824
Lewis, Michael & Elizabeth, 209 Butternut Dr.(Courtney, Alex)...................933-7559

Lewis, Nora, 2 Valentine Ln..929-2264
Lienesch, Michael, & Ann Baker, 72 Dogwood Dr.(Nicholas)........................929-8637
Linden, Carol A., 2704 Farthing St., Durham 27704....................................
Lindquist, David & Margaret (Maggie), 1520 Arboretum Dr.(Lisbet, Erik)...........933-0008
Lindsay, Robert & Elizabeth (Libby), 904 King's Mill Rd.........................942-6136
Lioret, Kent & June, 102 S. Christopher Rd...942-1742
Liptzin, Myron, c/o Student Health Service, Bldg. 469-H, UNC-CH..................967-5186
Little, James & Sylvia, 110 Ridge Ln.(Margaret, Cathy, Ann Marie)...............942-5023
Liverance, Bert & Mary Lou, 700 Kensington Dr.(Tom)............................929-8784
Lloyd, Evelyn, 111 N. Churton St., Hillsborough 27278............................732-2538
Lockerbie, Donald & Belinda, 118 Summerlin Dr.(Brittany)........................929-3038
Lockerbie, Kevin & Kimberly, 247 Kepley Rd..929-0631
Loeffler, Carol, 317 Wesley Dr..967-7692
Logan, Kathryn, 6332 Douglas St., Pittsburgh, PA 15217......................412/422-4221
London, Lawrence & Dewey, 217 Hillsborough St....................................942-1692
Long, Rachael, 20 Hayes Rd..968-0412
Lospinuso, Margaret, 7404 Abron Dr., Durham 27713..............................544-3255
Love, Spencie: see EPPS, Garrett
Loveland, George, 7-A Bolin Heights...929-4112
Lucas, Charles I., 304 S. Columbia St..
Ludington, C. Townsend & Jane 713 Shadylawn Rd.(David, Charles, James, Sarah).....942-7006
Lund, Mark & Donna, 2525 Booker Creek Rd., Apt. 15-A.(Mark, Jr.)..................
Lunde, Anders & Eleanor, 1120 Sourwood Dr.(Anne Louisa).........................929-3388
Lusth, John & Mary, Rt. 5, Box 116, Charlie Tew Ct., Hillsborough..27278..........
Lutton, Marilyn, 509 Craige, UNC-CH...933-7138
Luxon, Norval & Ermina, 27 Mt. Bolus Rd..942-2452
Lyall, Gordon & Dorothy, 2919 St. Charles Ave., Christ Church, New Orleans 70115.
Lycan, William & Mary, 415 Wesley Dr.(Katherine).................................967-0669
Lyon, Milly, 266 Severin St...929-3834
Lyons, Clifford & Gladys, 716 Greenwood Rd.......................................942-3337
Lyons, Mary, 1300 Carol Woods..942-4465

- M -

Maass, Nancy, 251 Cobb, UNC-CH...933-8018
Mabie, Peter & Jenny, 1937 Fireside Dr.(Stuart, Becka, Anna, Benjamin)...........942-8824
MacDonald, Margaret (Peg), 308 Laurel Hill Rd....................................967-5005
MacIntyre, Alan & Marguerite, 900 Stagecoach Rd.(Margo, Lynn)....................968-6868
Macauley, Michael (Mike) & Barbara, 318 McCauley St., #4.........................967-3998
Mace, Dana, 1605 Ephesus Church Rd.(Alex, Benjy, Lesley Jane)....................967-1102
Mack, Sara, 128 Milton Ave.(Richard & Anne Amis).................................967-4413
Mackey, William F. & Cecilia, 214 Old Forest Creek Dr.(Melinda,Katie,Amy)........967-6212
Macomson, Mollie, J-14 Woodbridge Apts., Carrboro 27510.(Tatum)..................967-9652
Madry, Scott & Sarah, 101 Oleander Dr., Carrboro 27510 (Adrienne)...............942-5825
Maginn, Vincent & Jane, 1112 Sourwood Circle.(Vincent Matthew)..................929-6841
Mallard, Agnes: see CROMARTIE, John
Mallon, Michael (Mike), 1312 Leclair St...929-5946
Malone, E.T., Jr. (Ted) & Lynda, 103 Carl Dr., Rt. 4.(Anna, Ned).................929-2858
Malone-Trahey, Arabella, & Tom Trahey, 17 Spring Garden Apts....................968-4530
Mangum, Bobby & Dana. 4307 Chapel Hill Rd., Durham 27707.........................493-5774
Manly, David & Dillon, 300-C Mason Farm Rd.......................................933-9778
Mann, Penny, 1221 SE 17th St., Portland, OR 97214............................503/232-4062
Manning, Betsy, Mint Springs Rd...942-3853

Marchese, Roberta, 113 Lexington Circle..967-8506
Markle, Nancy, #1 Georgetown Row, 318 McCauley St................................929-3992
Marsh, Mudge, 328 Forbush Mtn. Dr..929-8612
Martikainen, Helen, PO Box 3059 (14-F Stratford Hills Apts.)....................967-7458
Martin, Alex, 103 Barnhill Pl.(Hilary, Christina)..................................929-0122
Martin, Donald W., 330 Wesley Dr.,(Chad)..967-1875
Martin, Kenneth (Ken) & Virginia (Ginny), 2449 Honeysuckle Rd................967-3077
Martin, Michael & Farley, #34 Fearrington Post, Pittsboro 27312.(Michael Cody)...942-6562
Martin, Sophie, 519 Senlac Rd..968-5326
Martin, Stuart B., A-3 Graham Ct. Apts., 233-235 McCauley St....................929-5130
Mason, Chip & Joanna, 1 Durbin Pl., Durham 27705..................................383-0157
Mason, Elizabeth, 3200 Carol Woods..942-3050
Mason, Robert (Bob) & Shirley, Rt. 1, Box 190-A....................................967-3364
Massengale, Rosalie, 7 Cobb Terrace..942-1890
Massengale, Thomas & Page, 1503 Arboretum Dr.(Brooke, David, Alexander, Laurin)...929-2563
Masterton, Meta, 3100 Carol Woods..967-3800
Matson, Steve & Martha, 105 Spring Valley Rd., Carrboro 27510.(Timothy, Abigail).967-6634
Matteson, Stephen & Mary Ann, 423 Westwood Dr.(Stephen, Jr., Anne, Peter)........929-4365
Matthews, Harriet, 440 Fairoaks Circle.(David)......................................929-0637
Matthews, Joseph & Mary, 1009 Highland Woods..942-4891
Mayer, Danny, 2473 Foxwood Dr..942-7046
Mayfield, Bob & Lee, 609 Churchill Dr.(Laura, Jessee)............................929-2278
McAdams, Timothy (Tim) & Kathy, 411 Landerwood Ln.(Robin, Julia)................942-2908
McAllister, Gray, PO Box 864..929-1301
McAllister, H.C. (Mac), #3 Mint Springs Rd..942-3381
McCarthy, Evelyn B., 201 Marilyn Ln...967-6188
McCauley, Marvin W., PO Box 144..929-2866
McClister, Ptoebe, 409 North St.(Michael, Jenny)...................................
McClure, Bobbie, Rt. 3, Box 222-A, Apex 27502.......................................362-5190
McCombs, Kim, 653 Morrison, UNC-CH..933-4115
McConahay, Mary, Rt. 8, Box 68...942-5030
McConnell, Molly, 64 Davie Circle..929-1208
McCormack, Parrish, PO Box 6632, College Station, Durham 27708..................684-3796
McCormick, Margaret, 2109 Carol Woods...942-2275
McCoy, Ina, 16-D Booker Creek Apts...967-7471
McCoy, Rebecca, 14 Lanark Rd...929-6428
McCoy, Susan, PO Box 886..
McCracken, Tom & Marcia, 218 Kenston Ct., PO Box 466, Geneva, IL 60134.......312/272-4475
McCrory, Michael & Joellyn, Rt. 2, Box 345-A.(Michael, Lindsay)..................967-5803
McDonald, Betty Sue, 77 Willow Terrace..929-3023
McDonald, Cynthia Ann, 1485 Ephesus Church Rd..929-7649
McDonald, Susan M., 6 Heather Ct.(Andrea, Kimberly)................................942-1047
McDuffee, Robert B., 1709 Smith Level Rd.(Laura)...................................929-6074
McFadden, Janice, 118 Carol St., Carrboro 27510.....................................967-3830
McFee, Michael & Belinda, 2514 Pickett Rd., Durham 27705.(Philip)................493-4698
McGaghie, William (Bill) & Pam, 112 East Village Ln.(Michael, Kathleen)..........967-4430
McIlwain, Gail McLeod, 114 Meadowbrook Dr..929-9532
McKay, Martha, 1078 Nichols St., Raleigh 27605......................................834-5121
McKee, Beth, K-7 The Villages, Carrboro 27510 (Molly)..............................
McKeel, Richard, 304 E. Franklin St...942-2955
McKenzie, Burt & Nancy, 302 Carl Dr. (Eddie, Laura)................................967-6155
McKnight, Petey Bailey, 37 W. Dartmouth Rd., Kansas City, MO 64113..............
McLaughlin, Michael (Mike) & Noel, 109 Eastwood Lake Dr...........................942-2473
McLeod, Gail: see McILWAIN, Gail McLeod
McMillan, Campbell & Florence, 408 Ridgecrest Dr.(Bridget, Wendy)................942-2474

D-16

McMillan, Dougald, & Laura Murphy, 708 Greenwood Rd.(Dougald & Jennifer McMillan,
   Kate Murphy-McMillan, Cecelia Claire Murphy-McMillan).edit 1577..................942-8073
McMullan, Barbara, 200 E. Poplar St., Carrboro 27510.(Margaret)...................967-7129
McMurry, Jane, 1417 Country Club Rd., Wilmington 28403.(Winifred, Allison).......
McNamara, Dan, 8964 Tarrytown Dr., Richmond, VA 23229.............................
McNary, Kenneth & Janet, Rt. 7, Box 663-B...929-3173
McNeil, Gail, 4 Dartford Ct...929-5485
McVaugh, Michael & Julia, 379 Tenney Circle.......................................967-1191
Meegan, Janet, 223 Forbush Mountain Rd..942-8963
Meierdierck, Dorothy, 203 W. Rosemary St.(Marie, Alfred)..........................942-4559
Meldahl, Virginia, 105 S. Peak Dr., Carrboro 27510...............................942-1662
Meredith, Janet N., 3 Oakwood Dr..929-3263
Merritt, Marjorie I., 58 Polks Landing..933-0648
Merten, David F., Jr., & Barbara, 201 Longwood Dr.(Kate, Betsy, Pete, Rob)........489-6937
Metcalfe, Donna: see DUCEY, Mitchell
Metzloff, Tom & Nancy, 3523 Racine St., Durham 27707 (Emily, Christopher).......489-1753
Meyer, George W. & Euva, 1118 Sourwood Dr...942-7053
Meyer, George W., Jr., & Paula, 1516 Arboretum Dr.,(Wright, Helen)................967-7944
Meyer, John, & Susan, 3623 Barcelona Ave., Durham 27707.(Jordan).................489-7934
Meyer, Phil & Sue, 610 Croom St.(Missy, Sarah)....................................933-0605
Miles, Duke, 2536 Wrightwood Ave., Durham 27705..................................493-4017
Miller, *Bruce: see HUFF, Anne
Miller, Charles, & Lisa Fischbeck, 313 Granville Rd...............................929-7267
Miller, Claudius & Sally, Fearrington Village, 147 Tinderwood, Pittsboro 27312...542-5811
Miller, David, 616-A Hibbard Dr...933-5883
Miller, Eileen, 16 Banbury Ln...
Miller, Ellen, 125 Carol Woods..942-4946
Miller, O. Phil, Dr., Rt. 5, Box 178-B..
Miller, Robert (Bob), 413 Morgan Creek Rd..968-3632
Mills, Colleen C., 2461 Wayfarer Ct...942-7232
Mitchell, Sara: see EDWARDS, Phil
Mitterling, John, 321 W. Cameron Ave..933-5112
Moe, Jeffrey, Rt. 6, #604 Paddock Dr., Raleigh 27612..............................
Moffie, Robert & Tracey, 17 Weybridge Pl..
Molpus, Margaret, Rt. 7, Box 90, Durham 27707....................................489-5825
Monroe, Howard, Jr., 18 Frances St..942-0616
Montague, Beth, 501-A Caswell Rd..929-8162
Mooers, Frank & Helen, 1820 S. Lakeshore Dr.......................................967-5205
Moore, Deborah, 217 Greene St., #4..
Moore, Joseph & Alice, 404 Lyons Rd. (Laura, Kelly)..............................967-3729
Moore, Lawrence (Larry), & Minnie Lewis, 1311 LeClair St. (Kathryn, Marianne).....929-6345
Moore, Natalie (Lee), 412 Thornwood Rd..942-7267
Moore, Richard, 1825 White Oak Rd, Raleigh 27608.................................833-7411
Moore, Thaddeus (Ted) & Mary, 223 Hillcrest Circle.(Thad, Alexander).............929-2336
Morgan, George, 128-C Purefoy Rd..929-5326
Morris, Glenn & Judy 405 Landerwood Ln.(Allison, Alexandra)......................929-6795
Morris, Richard & Mary Ann, King's Mill Rd.(Karen, David)........................933-9392
Morris, Richard & Julie, 112 Hidden Valley Dr.(Zachary)..........................967-1519
Morrison, Olga W., 6 Maxwell Rd...929-7380
Moskal, Jeanne, 420 Ridgefield Rd...929-1025
Moulton, Dorothy, 138 Carol Woods...929-8373
Mowry, Katherine (Kay), 132 Carol Woods...942-1216
Mullikin, Kent & Miriam, 101 Windsor Pl.(Anna, Sally)............................929-1946
Munford, McKay, 1617-C Old Oxford Rd..
Munn, Dan & Mia, 179 Fearrington Post, Pittsboro 27312.(Philip)..................542-5338

D-17

Murph, Jeffrey, Virginia Theological Seminary, Seminary PO, Alexandria, VA 22304
Murphy, Andy, 203 Grimes, UNC-CH...933-8721
Murphy, Anne, 800 Pittsboro Rd.(Laura, Rachel)...................................942-3471
Murphy, Daniel & Mary, 1304 Willow Dr...968-3322
Murphy, Laura: see McMILLAN, Dougald
Murphy, Susan, Rt. 8, Box 110 (Sean, Matthew)...................................942-3773
Murray, Doug, 213 Grove Ave., Huntsville, AL 35801...............................
Myers, John L., 1238 C. St., NE, Washington, DC 20003...........................
Myers, Robert & Marjorie, 90 Cedar Hills Circle.(Anne)..........................942-5690
Mynatt, Mr. & Mrs. Joe, 211 Conner Dr., #17.....................................967-2362

- N -

Nance, Frederick (Rick) & Jean, 102 Huntington Dr.(Taylor, Courtney).............967-2823
Nash, David, PO Box 374...942-4880
Navey, Susan, 217 Northampton Terrace...967-9682
Nayfeh, Gigi, 703 Kensington Dr...929-9376
Ndoboli, Fred, 530 Craige, UNC-CH...
Neacsu, Michael & Carrie, I-9 Carolina Apts., Carrboro 27510....................933-9387
Neary, Howard & Helen, 42-E Stratford Hills Apts.(Michele)......................929-3663
Nelson, John & Nancy, 1507 Lamont Ct..942-4535
Nestor, Bryan & Susan, 0-12 Colony Apts...942-2036
Neville, Everett, 4-M Estes Park Apts., Carrboro 27510..........................968-8314
Neville, John, PO Box 26853, Raleigh 27611......................................833-7976
New, Steven & Caterri, 1006 Demerius St., Durham 27701..........................682-7850
Newton, Mike, 104 W. Poplar Ave., Carrboro 27510................................
Nichols, Carol, 248 Nature Trail..929-9677
Nicholson, Marjorie, Rt. 5, Box 182...929-2246
Nicholson, Don, Jr., 502 Pritchard Ave.(Cory)...................................929-0151
Nicholson, Garret & Liz, 3 Brandon Rd.(Connor, Kate, Emma)......................942-3541
Nicholson, Mike, Rt. 5, Box 182...967-6806
Nisbet, Debbie, 22 Oak Dr., Durham 27707.(Thomas, William, John).................489-7845
Nordstrom, Everett & Mary, 1914 White Plains Rd.................................942-3822
Norgren, Fran, 288 Second St. South, Naples, FL 33940.......................813/263-4114
Northup, Amy, 10825 Bexhill Dr., Raleigh 27606..................................469-1936
Nugent, Richard & Cathy, 443 Ridgefield Rd.(Stephanie, Erik, Benjamin)..........929-7018
Nuzum, Tom & Jean, 213 N. Boundary St.(Christine, Henry)........................929-8627
Nye, Kemp & Nancy, PO Box 1003..942-6360

- O -

O'Briant, Neal, 701 Coventry Ct., Raleigh 27609.................................
O'Brien, Daintry, 101-A Bolinwood Apts..929-0592
O'Shea, Bill, 213 F. Franklin St., #32..942-5435
Oates, Kathy, 506 N. Greensboro St., #32, Carrboro 27310........................
Oliver, Randolph & Mary, Rt. 7, Box 299-D, George King Rd., Durham 27707.........
Ollis, David & Marcia (Marcy), 2 Foxridge Rd.(Andrew, Mark, Stephen, Matthew).....968-4020
Otis, Christine C., 5911 Third St., S., St. Petersburg, FL 33705................

Pagano, Joseph & Nancy Reynolds, 114 Laurel Hill Rd.............................942-2936
Page, Ellis B. & Elizabeth, 110 Oakstone Dr...................................929-8508
Page, Elizabeth Bass, 105 S. Boundary St.......................................942-3594
Paine, Ruth, 26 Mt. Bolus Rd...929-1419
Palmer, Chris, 108-B Sue Ann Ct., Carrboro 27510...............................
Parish, Havner & Isabel, 260 Fearrington, Pittsboro 27312......................542-5863
Parker, Helen B., PO Box 2001, Southern Pines 28387............................692-4768
Parker, David, 12-K Royal Park Apts., Carrboro 27510...........................
Parker, Tania, Rt. 7, Box 8-B.(Ember)..967-3143
Parker, William & Athena, 264 Parker Rd..933-7986
Parks, Jane, N-10 Woodbridge Apts., Carrboro 27510.............................968-8347
Parks, Mr. & Mrs. John, PO Box 2563, 27515.....................................
Parmentier, A.J. (Bud) & Mary Ann, 6618 Falconbridge Rd........................544-4777
Parnell, Jane, 106-A Pleasant Dr., Carrboro 27510..............................929-7036
Pasi, Deepak & Carla, 100 Gary Rd., Carrboro 27510.(Travis Wolfe)..............967-3226
Pate, James & Pamela, Rt. 2, Box 485-B, Cedronella Rd.(Jim, Branham)...........383-5906
Patrick, Michael W. & Margaret Kemper, Rt. 4, Box 354..........................929-4948
Patrick, Vincente, 115 Robin Road..942-3572
Patterson, Sarah (Sally), 111 Pine Hill Dr., Carrboro 27510....................929-4974
Patterson, Julia (Bootsie), 511 Senlac Rd......................................968-3701
Patterson, Mary, 116 Carol Woods...942-3693
Patton, Carlotta, 614 E. Franklin St...942-3724
Pauk, Elizabeth, Rt. 1, Box 101-B4, Hurdle Mills, NC 27541.....................732-6649
Pavlik, Philip, 104 Carr St...942-8065
Pearce, Ann Stuart, 202 Aycock, UNC-CH...933-1676
Pearson, Jackie, 212-4 Pinegate Circle...489-9299
Peck, Joan G., 7 Dartford Ct...493-8241
Pedersen, Lee & Barbara, 28 Oakwood Dr...929-3301
Pegg, Bill & Susan, 115 Pitch Pine Lane.(Tyler)................................933-8668
Pegg, C.H. & Eleanor, 32 Mt. Bolus Rd..942-4522
Peirce, Jeffrey & Jo, 906 King's Mill Rd.(Shayn, Leye).........................967-8357
Pendergrass, Frances, Rt. 4, Box 409,..942-4546
Penniall, Ralph & Mary, 103 Round Hill Rd......................................942-2724
Pennington, Liz, PO Box 7001, Duke Sta., Durham 27708..........................684-1678
Perkins, Greg, 2933 Buckingham Rd., Durham 27707.(Sean)........................489-1509
Pettito, Jenny Burns, 707-A Wellington Dr......................................967-2874
Pfaff, David, 321 W. Cameron Ave...968-9305
Pfaff, Richard & Margaret (Margie), 334 Wesley Dr..............................942-1309
Phay, Mr. & Mrs. Robert, 313 Birch Circle......................................942-5997
Philips, Josept & Sara, Rt. 12, Box 50...942-3524
Philips, Pat, Apt. 49 Brighton Square, Carrboro 27510..........................
Phillips, Robert (Bob) & Christine Erskine, 206 Ridgecrest Dr.(Anna, Fran, Betsy).967-8407
Pilkington, Theo & Janet, 2932 Ridge Rd., Durham 27705.(Patrick)...............489-5540
Pillsbury, Rick & Sally, 111 Burnwood Ct.(Matthew, Benjamin, Thomas)...........968-8337
Pindell, Stephen, 120 Ashe Ave., Raleigh 27605.................................
Pinnix, David Michael, 39 Old East, UNC-CH.....................................933-6055
Piper, Derrell & Jean, H-9 Carolina Apts., Carrboro 27510......................942-0136
Pipkin, Michael & Barbara, 806 Churchill Dr.(David)............................929-5923
Piso, Michael & Rebecca, 314-E Cheswick Pl, Cary 27511.........................
Pitts, Jeff, 1707 Bivins, Durham 27707...
Plaisance, Pat, Rt. 4, #9 Lake Village...967-3362
Plymire, James, PO Box 3700, 27515...942-1165

Podger, Kenneth & Karen, 2531 Booker Creek Rd.(Kelly, Kristen)...................967-6379
Pogoloff, Stephen & Christina, 904 1/2 Dacian Ave., Durham 27701.(Eliz., Michael)682-7678
Poole, Gary & Edie, 201 Westbrook Dr., Apt. D-16, Carrboro 27510.................929-0703
Popio, Kenneth, & Melody Harrison, 324 W. University Dr.(Nicholas)................967-7765
Popkin, Carol, 502 1/2 Dogwood Dr...942-7827
Porter, Carol Q., 49 Circle Dr..929-9012
Porter, Donald & Carrie, F-3 Colony Woods Apts..................................
Porter, Harry & Flo, 1101 Carol Woods...967-2567
Potts, Fanny, 1317 Carol Woods..967-4244
Potts, Jennifer, 1013 Wells St., Durham 27707-1621..............................
Powell, Charles & Carolyn, 2446 Honeysuckle Rd..................................929-3507
Powell, Hank & Maggie, Rt. 2, Box 220, Mebane 27401.............................563-3012
Powell, Lisa K., 342 Cobblestone Ct...967-1793
Prescott, Ann, 421 Granville Rd.(Karen, Lorinne)................................967-1629
Prettyman, Virginia, 309 Country Club Rd..967-4437
Prigden, Genie, 211 Henderson St..968-0203
Pringle, John & Elizabeth (Betsy), 636 Rock Creek Rd.(John, Laura, Joseph,Charles)929-9713
Prouty, William, 603 Airport Rd., 1-D...
Pulliam. Charles & Linda, 863 Weaver Dairy Rd.(Noel)............................942-7348

-- Q -

Queen, Anne, Rt. 4, Box 73, Canton 28716..................................704/648-5453
Quinn, Suzanne, 1102 Willow Dr.(Karen, Kathleen, & Kristin Uebele)...............968-4316
Quinn, Wylie S.(Van), & Margaret (Peggy), 127 Hunter's Ridge Rd.(Nathaniel, Molly)933-3116

- R -

Rabb, Walter & Amy, 202 Hillcrest Rd..942-5789
Rains, Irene (Renie), PO Box 306..942-1791
Ramirez, Ana, 1605 Ephesus Church Rd..967-1102
Raney, Beverly & Carolyn, PO Box 2467, 27515....................................942-3764
Raney, Thomas, PO Box 2421, 27515...967-4465
Rao, Ennio, 142 Loblolly Ln...933-9630
Rasmussen, Ken, 313 Purefoy Rd..967-1225
Read, Kenneth & Joann (Jody), Edgewood Rd.......................................933-6450
Reckford, Joe, 729 E. Franklin St...942-3723
Reed, John & Dale, 126 Mallette St.(Elisabeth, Sarah)...........................929-6924
Rees, Philip & Margaret (Peg), 503 Otey's Rd.(David, Peter).....................929-2493
Reeves, Elizabeth, 1 Point Prospect...967-3443
Reinhardt, Brian, 477 N. Ashe St., Southern Pines 27387.........................
Reist, Pete & Jan, 205 Glenhill Lane.(Adam, Sophie).............................929-6681
Reiter, Lizette, 607 Hillsborough Rd., Carrboro 27510...........................967-4927
Remington, Laura, 624 Ehringhaus, UNC-CH..933-3160
Reynolds, Joe & Chris, 101 Webb Dr., Carrboro 27510.............................968-8290
Rezner, Lelia, 105 Hamilton Rd..929-4818
Richards, Mary Margaret, 105 Stinson St...942-7098
Richardson, Alexander, 105 Stone's Throw, Polks Landing.........................929-3042
Ricker, Evelyn, 63 Tar Heel Mobile Ct., 1200 Airport Rd.........................929-9953
Riddle, Michael A., 2524-B Booker Creek Rd......................................933-7788
Riggall, Dan & Fran, 501 Westover Dr., Monroe 28110.(Justin)................704/289-9243

- S -

Schliebe, Eric & Barbara, 140 Stateside Dr.(Erich, Mary, Karl, Elizabeth)........967-3070
Schliff, Henry, Jr. & Michal, 24 East Dr.(Henry, III)..............................942-7313
Schlitt, Tom & Rara, 2518-A Milwood Ct..942-0248
Schnorrenberg, David, 321 W. Cameron Ave..968-9305
Schofield, Edward & Martha, 303 Colony Woods Dr.................................929-5560
Scholl, Diana, Rt. 7, Box 306.(Juliana)...933-0723
Schumann, Cathy, Rt. 7, Old Lystra Rd...929-1494
Schunior, Charles & Anne Carter, 311 Carol St., Carrboro 27510.(Justi, Emily)....929-5123
Schutz, John & Barbara, 311 Birch Circle..942-3696
Scott, Walter, 1905 Apex Highway, Durham 27707....................................
Scully, Robert & Gabrielle, 701 Emory Dr.(Jennifer, Eleanor)....................967-7626
Seate, Mary Ellen, 53 Cedar Terrace Rd..933-6480
Seaton, Joseph & Karen, 56 Polks Landing...933-9515
Sechriest, Mary P., 10-F Sharon Heights Apts....................................967-7983
Sechriest, Stuart & Carolyn, 14 Mt. Bolus Rd....................................942-7214
Selden, Emily, 1817 S. Lakeshore Dr...942-6469
Sellet, Lucien & Susan, 1404 Arboretum Dr.......................................967-4895
Shafer, Robert & Paquita, 12 Banbury Ln...942-4706
Shaffer, Charles & Charlotte, 716 Gimghoul Rd...................................967-2406
Shahady, Tom & Trude, 112-A W. Poplar Ave., Carrboro 27510........................
Sharpe, John L., III, PO Box 4682, Duke Sta., Durham 27706.......................688-2135
Sharpless, Richard (Dick) & Jean, PO Box 3471, 27515............................967-8766
Sharrock, Cindy, Rt. 7, Box 619..933-8505
Shea, Don & Goldie, 102 Northwood Dr..929-9919
Shearer, Mr. & Mrs. Kenneth, 401 Forest Ct., Carrboro 27510.....................929-5687
Shelburne, Brian, D-3 Camelot Village...942-3230
Sheldon, George & Ruth Guy, 709 Greenwood Rd....................................967-4066
Shene, Mary Ellen, C-6 Tar Heel Manor Apts., Carrboro 27510.....................942-6717
Shepherd, Hazel, 307 Gary Rd., Carrboro 27510...................................933-7703
Sheridan, Sharon, 405 Ruffin, UNC-CH..933-5735
Shetland, Margaret L., 1318 Carol Woods...942-3346
Shipman, Susan I., 1801 The Oaks (Charlie, Katherine)...........................929-5213
Shipp, Kenneth (Ken), 3646 Crystal Ct., Durham 27705............................477-3295
Shugart, Sanford (Sandy) & Jane, 200 Glen Eden, Durham 27713....................544-4046
Shull, Dee Ann, 106-A Barnes St., Carrboro 27510................................966-2388
Simpson, Lexie, #3 Penick Ln.(Hayes, Benjamin)..................................929-4198
Sisco, Paul, 6515 English Oaks Dr., Raleigh 27609.................................
Sitterson, J. Carlyle & Nancy, 217 Hillcrest Circle.............................929-2428
Skinner, Margaret, 1008 Dawes St.(DeLacey Ann)..................................942-7528
Skinner, Sally, 902 Dawes St..942-4694
Slater, Herschel & Gladys, 1310 Willow Dr.......................................929-5889
Slaughter, Jean, 150 Windsor Circle.(Amy).......................................968-8066
Slayton, William (Bill), 728 Tinkerbell Rd......................................929-6692
Smallegan, Marian, 18-H Stratford Hills Apts....................................929-4735
Smart, Max & Dawn, PO Box 2821, 27515...942-0702
Smathers, Micki, 5-B Royal Park Apts., Carrboro 27510...........................933-3086
Smelzer, Timothy & Anne Marie (Mimi), 625 F. Franklin St.(Andrea, Peter)........929-5681
Smiley, Lynn: see GILLIGAN, Peter
Smith, Lee: see CROWTHER, Hal
Smith, Michael & Mary Dodge, 106 Greenfield Rd.(Andrew, Patrick, Daniel)........929-9800
Smith, Phyllis, 301-2 Pinegate Circle..
Smith, Bob & Paula, #247 Fearrington Post, Pittsboro 27312......................542-4862
Smith, Mr. & Mrs. Spencer A., #9 Beech Tr., Durham 27705........................489-1001
Snow, Henrietta, PO Box 2001, Southern Pines 28387
Snyder, Susan, C-9 Carolina Apts., Carrboro 27510...............................942-2517

Solovieff, Gregory, Rt. 2, Box 500...383-7239
Sowers, Lynn, Rt. 9, Box 546-C..967-7914
Spangler, John & Bes, 702 N. Blount St., Raleigh 27604.(Heywood).................839-1746
Sparger, Celia, 94 Hamilton Rd..929-6379
Sparks, Martha, 15 Boothe Hill, Rt. 9...967-3416
Sparling, Fred & Joyce, 303 Weaver Rd.(Betsey, Mark)..............................942-1567
Sparrow, Michael, Rt. 1, Box 204, Pittsboro 27312.................................929-4526
Speas, Frances: see KOHUT, Frances
Spinelli, Christine V., 116 High St., Carrboro 27510..............................942-7504
Sprenger, Alice, 104 Juniper Place..493-5300
Stainback, Dianne, G-11 Village Green...942-2336
Stanford, David & Ann, 106 Walden Dr., Carrboro 27510.(Ben).......................933-9222
Stanford, Don C., PO Box 425..967-5652
Stanley, Liz, 224 Kenan, UNC-CH...933-1455
Stapleton, Jack & Anne, 205 Gary Rd., Carrboro 27510.(Samuel, Molly)..............942-8303
Steck, Fred & Genie, 2004 S. Lake Shore Dr..967-5230
Stedman, Donald & Helen, Rt. 5, Box 330-B...967-7678
Stedman, Cary & Susan, PO Box 1205, Pittsboro 27312.(Jonathan)....................933-6960
Steele, Cheryl, 171 Kingston Dr. (Charles)..929-0430
Steele, Diana, 1207 Mason Farm Rd...929-8922
Steele, George & Katherine, 205 W. University Dr.(Katherine)......................968-8239
Stenberg, Craig & DeeAnn, 108-A Weatherstone Dr.(Allison, Philip).................967-7211
Stephenson, Daniel, Rt. 11, Box 3000, Pine Grove Trailer Pk.......................
Stephenson, Suzanne, 910 Emory Dr.(Kim, Kristi, Laura, Lisa)......................968-1040
Stevens, Edith, 448 Northside Dr.(Toby)...967-5053
Stevens, Hazel: see SHEPHERD, Hazel
Stewart, William & Judy, 449 Lakeshore Lane.......................................929-6371
Stiles, Gary & Jane, 2463 Foxwood Dr.(Heather, Wendy).............................929-9117
Stiles, George & Judy, 633 Arlington St.(Buddy, Jonathan).........................929-8590
Stinnett, Sandra, 23 East Dr..929-3745
Stone, Eleanore (Ruth), 2920 Chapel Hill Rd., Apt. 39-D, Durham 27707.(Holly)....493-3181
Stone, Madolene, 407-A Smith Ave..967-7620
Stoudemire, Sterling & Mary Arthur, 712 Gimghoul Rd...............................942-3468
Stout, Robert, 213 N. Melville St., Graham 27253..................................227-0362
Strand, Evelyn (Lyn), 1800 Williamsburg Way, Apt. 11-D, Durham 27707.............383-9295
Straughan, Chris & Dulcie, 500 Woodcroft Pkwy, 7-B Homeplace, Durham 27703(David).493-1126
Strawn, Steve & Laura, 18-A Sharon Heights Apts...................................967-8782
Stribling, Catherine, 111 N. Estes Dr...967-1306
Strother, Lois, 1429 Airport Rd...929-5463
Stroud, Sue, Rt. 10, Box 305-C., Raleigh 27603....................................
Stufflebeam, Shawn C., 728 Morrison, UNC-CH.......................................933-4091
Stynes, Kenneth & Joan, 210 Celeste Circle (Aran, Brian, Christopher).............544-3251
Sullivan, Bernadine, 615 E. Rosemary St...942-2765
Sullivan, Robert (Rob) & Kim, 294 Highview Dr.(Loring, Lee).......................967-7568
Sutherland, Suzanne, 402 Wesley Dr..967-9261
Suttenfield, Virginia, Rt. 12, Box 76, Farrington Rd..............................967-5783
Swank, Mary, 237-A Jackson Circle (Anna, Sophie)+.................................933-6734
Swanson, Susan, 15 Dartford Ct..493-8072
Sweeney, Thomas & Ruth Ellen, 411 Highview Dr.(Daniel, Jennifer)..................929-5799
Swenberg, James & Sandra, 111 Stoneridge Dr.(Dan, Heather)........................967-7416
Swetlicke, Joyce, 208 Craige, UNC-CH..933-7041
Sykes, John Collins, III, 216 Lewis, UNC-CH.......................................933-1548
Szymanski, Cathy, 11-A Royal Park Apts., Carrboro 27510...........................942-6461

Taggart, Eleanor & Elsie, 110 Larkspur Circle, Durham 27713.....................544-2835
Talbot, Addison & Ann, 375 Tenney Circle...929-7675
Tate, Knox & Stella Waugh, 407 Morgan Creek Rd.(Elizabeth Grew)....................929-5915
Taylor, Betsy, 422 Ridgefield Rd..967-7697
Taylor, Catherine S. & James, 4413 Bracada Dr., Durham 27705.(William, Andrew)...383-8885
Taylor, Alice Lee, 2111 Carol Woods...967-5233
Taylor, James & Lib, Fern Ln..942-4577
Taylor, Susan, 2508 Millwood Ct.(Julia)...967-6742
Taylor, Leslie L., PO Box 210, Smithfield 27577.....................................
Taylor, Louise, 4 Banbury Ln..967-4700
Taylor, Marguerite (Cricket), 71 Dogwood Acres Dr..................................933-7461
Taylor, N.Ferebee, 3 The Glen...967-4144
Taylor, Richard & Karen, Rt. 7, Box 282.(Chloe).....................................942-1426
Taylor, Robert & Barry Murrill, Rt. 7, Box 321.(Charles Carr)......................933-9497
Taylor, Ronald & Cynthia, Rt. 4, Box 537..929-4424
Taylor, Sarah, 2401 Northrop Ave., #2, Sacramento, CA 95825...................916/488-2254
Teachey, Tracy, 1102-B W. Main St., Carrboro 27510..................................
Terhune, Ramsey & Sarah, 518 North St.(Dylan, Graham)..............................929-6127
Thegze, Nancy, 107 Fieldstone Ct..929-7861
Thomas, Everett, PO Box 412...929-2081
Thomas, Henry & Linda, PO Box 205 Fearrington, Pittsboro 27312 (Elizabeth,Jordan)542-5405
Thomas, Mr. & Mrs. Henry C., Sr., 103 Pine Lane.....................................
Thomas, Lee, 110 Barbee Ct., Carrboro 27510...968-8083
Thomas, Patricia, 501 North St..942-6720
Thomas, Vera, Rt. 2, Box 16, Woodcrest Trailer Ct...................................933-8419
Thompson, Corleen, 1103 S. Columbia St..942-2809
Thompson, Richard M., & Joan, 116 Essex Dr..967-7348
Thompson, Mr & Mrs. Robert, 307 Yorktown Dr...967-5318
Thompson, Tommy & Susan, 401-B Coolidge St.(Hannah Byrum)...........................967-4270
Thorpe, Jean, PO Box 3154, 27515..967-0399
Tilden, Douglas & Roberta, 100 Crabapple Ln.(Drew, Christopher)....................489-4498
Tilly, Eben F., Jr. & Nancy, 628 Kensington Dr.(Jeb)...............................929-8880
Tilly, Eben F., Sr. & Elizabeth, 9 Banbury Ln......................................929-5545
Tilton, Charles S., 167 Carol Woods...929-8075
Timmons, Joan, 708 Tinkerbell Rd..942-1753
Tippett, Scott & Karen, 7-B Towne House Apts..929-4673
Todd, Rebecca, 2 Washington Sq. Village, Apt. 4-A, New York, NY 10012.(Anne).212/674-0951
Todd, Jacob (Jake) & Joyce, PO Box 983, Raleigh 27602.........................781-2799
Tolbert, PO Box 518...
Tolley, Jeannette, 110 Laurel Hill Rd...942-5754
Tostanoski, Ed, D-1 University Gardens Apts...
Trembley, Paul, PO Box 3602, 27515..
Trimble, Hazel, 232 Glandon Dr..942-3397
Trimble, Sally, 232 Glandon Dr..942-3397
Tukey, Melissa, 888-A Cedar Fork Tr.(Brendon)......................................929-2194
Tulbert, Mark. K.S., 728-B Grove Ave., Raleigh 27606...............................851-8021
Turchi, Boone & Janet, 700 Bradley Rd.(Francesca, Alex)............................942-6778
Turner, Susan, 605 Tinkerbell Rd..929-4824
Turner, Susan, 1202 Burning Tree Dr. (Courtney Gantt).............................967-4744
Tyson, Ruel & Martha, 743 E. Franklin St...929-3137
Tzavaras, Carrie, Rt. 2, Box 395, Hillsborough 27278...............................

Dee Turner - 968. 4475

3117 Sloane -

. do setpr
list medirf← fopr ←←←r "carolw"$locl .and. "¡"$dir

00101 Barnard, Margaret, 2204 Carol Woods.................................942-6709
00155 Blankenship, Margaret, 103 Carol Woods.............................942-2649
00168 Bond, Marjorie, 1111 Carol Woods..................................942-1997
00177 Bowman, Waldo & Virginia, 1313 Carol Woods........................942-5088
00218 Buchheister, Harriet, 819 Carol Woods Health Care Center..........967-3409
00251 Calverly, Eliza, Carol Woods Health Center........................
00259 Campbell, Tacy, Carol Woods Health Center, D-60...................929-4619
00285 Case, Harry & Elinor, 188 Carol Woods.............................967-4194
00320 Cherry, Robert, C-38 Carol Woods Health Center....................
00352 Cobb, Emma, 1102 Carol Woods......................................968-3501
00354 Cocke, Richard & Betty, 163 Carol Woods...........................929-2803
00359 Coker, Mary, 3204 Carol Woods.....................................942-2130
00372 Comtois, Joseph & Louise, 181 Carol Woods.........................942-2306
00388 Cooker, Mrs. T. Dickerson, 2215 Carol Woods.......................942-4584
00400 Corpening, Anne, 130 Carol Woods..................................942-8956
00405 Couch, John & Elser, 1109 Carol Woods.............................942-3097
00429 Crockford, Helen, 2118 Carol Woods................................942-2062
00459 Darley, Kathleen, Carol Woods Health Care Center..................929-5149
00485 Davis, Lois, 155 Carol Woods......................................968-8009
00526 DeVoe, Hazel, 182 Carol Woods.....................................967-4305
00613 Elder, Francis (Frank) & Virginia, 144 Carol Woods................942-1544
00628 Ensign, Marty, 1214 Carol Woods...................................967-0019
00734 Francis, Allen & Edith, 2105 Carol Woods..........................929-4190
00784 Givens, Margaret, 2201 Carol Woods................................942-6105
00922 Hartogensis, Laura, 115 Carol Woods...............................942-7826
00923 Hartzo, Dorothea H., 1208 Carol Woods.............................942-1686
00935 Hazlett, Mary Elizabeth (Ibby), 3114 Carol Woods..................942-3585
00948 Henderson, William (Will), 1307 Carol Woods.......................929-2466
00974 Highriter, Mildred, 2106 Carol Woods..............................929-1915
01113 Jones, Annie Lee, 3103 Carol Woods................................929-1665
01306 Lyons, Mary, 1300 Carol Woods 942-4465
01378 Masterton, Meta, 3100 Carol Woods.................................967-3800
01407 McCormick, Margaret, 2109 Carol Woods.............................942-2275
01503 Miller, Ellen, 125 Carol Woods....................................942-4946
01559 Moulton, Dorothy, 138 Carol Woods.................................929-8373
01560 Mowry, Kay, 132 Carol Woods.......................................942-1216
01743 Potts, Fanny, 1317 Carol Woods....................................967-4244
01815 Ring, Mary, Carol Woods Health Center.............................
01835 Robson, Charles (Pat) & Harriet, 119 Carol Woods..................967-3036
01960 Shetland, Margaret L., 1318 Carol Woods...........................942-3346
02105 Taylor, Alice Lee, 2111 Carol Woods...............................967-5233
02162 Tilton, Charles S., 167 Carol Woods...............................929-8075
02610 Von Storch, Anne B., 1205 Carol Woods.............................
02277 Webb, Louise, 2105 Carol Woods....................................929-2506
02368 Womack, Margaret, 3102 Carol Woods................................967-1147
02377 Woodward, Henry, 2218 Carol Woods.................................967-7814

Elena Watson   410 Whitehead Circle   Chapel Hill, NC 27
Denie & Fred Steck 3559 Springmoor Circle Raleigh

lidt←←st dir for "penmick←←←←ick"$locl .and. "¡"$dir
00009 Adams, Edward & Polly, PO Box 2001, Southern Pines 28387..............692-9598
00169 Boston, Margaret, PO Box 2001, Southern Pines 28387...................
00194 Broe, Helen, PO Box 2001, Southern Pines 28387.......................
00602 Edkins, Marie, PO Box 2001, Southern Pines 28387.....................

- U -

Uebele, Karen, Kathleen, & Kristin: see QUINN, Suzanne
Unger, Rosemary, PO Box 6473, Durham 27708.................................286-3749
Unks, Gerald, One Maple Dr...967-6604

- V -

Van Hoy, Milton, 104 Carr St...942-8065
Van Laanen, Dolph & Carolyn, 1 Penick Ln.......................................942-6526
Van Pelt, Kendrick & Carol, 8 Foxridge Rd.(Carolyn & Kendra)...................942-5266
Van Sant, Carolyn, 502 North St..929-3111
Vance, Rheba, 169 Hamilton Rd..942-3277
Varner, Barney & Vivian, 294 Azalea Dr.(Joshua, Miriam)........................933-6863
Vause, Chanee, 306 McCauley St...967-6673
Vesilind, P. Arne & Gail, 513 Lakeshore Ln.(Pam, Laurie, Steve)...............967-4654
Vieweager, Vivian, 3324 Rolling Hill Rd., Durham 27705........................493-6224
Vilas-Gooder, Sally, 3 Rocky Ridge Rd..929-5338
Vogler, Fred, 1010 Dawes St.(Robert)...929-1253
Vogler, Mary Frances, 40 Oakwood Dr..
Von Storch, Anne B., 1205 Carol Woods..

- W -

Wade, Rebekah, Rt. 3, Box 378, Mann's Chapel Rd.(Livia)........................933-8639
Wade, Livia, PO Box 17629, Guilford College, Greensboro 27410.................
Wagner, Sibyl: see WOFFORD, Adams
Wainwright, Geoffrey, 4011 W. Cornwallis Rd., Durham 27705....................
Walker, Lara, 836 Shady Lawn Rd..967-2080
Wallace, Carl & Diana, 140 Carolina Forest.(Jack, Brian, Will)................967-3693
Wallace, Patricia, 213 E. Franklin St, #5......................................968-1552
Walton, Randy, & Teri Ward, Rt. 3, Box 133, Durham 27713......................544-3581
   (Kathryn Ward-Walton, Heather Ward-Walton)
Ward, Jim & Elizabeth, 631 Tinkerbell Rd.(David, Karyn)........................968-8399
Ward, Mike & Trisha, 1506 1/2 Mason Farm Rd....................................933-7229
Ward, Susan T., 617 W. North St., Apt. E, Raleigh 27603.......................839-0178
Ward, Teri: see WALTON, Randy
Warden, James A., 609 Sugarberry Rd..942-5097
Warner, Susan, St. Jude's Ranch, Box 985, Boulder City, NV 89005..............
Warner, Seth & Emily, 2433 Wrightwood Ave., Durham 27705 (Susan, Sarah, Lawrence)489-3997
Warner, Sarah, Box 224, Colorado College, Colorado Springs, CO 80903..........
Warren, Caroline, 65 Hamilton Rd...942-5497
Warren, Charles & Patricia, 3119 Morningside Dr., Raleigh 27607...............781-9135
Warren, David & Marsha, 408 Lyons Rd.(Douglas, Jeffrey, Amy)..................942-2480
Warren, Joseph & Katherine, 115 Battle Lane....................................942-1660
Warren, Martha, 417 Lakeshore Ln...967-1501
Warren, Rebecca, 214 McCauley St...942-5497
Waterfall, Ann, 4115 Beechnut Lane, Durham 27707..............................489-7751
Watkins, Julia (Judy), 1708 Curtis Rd..942-7110
Watson, Charles & Masha, 134 Hunter's Ridge Rd.(Vanya, Misha, Ana)............933-8408

```
Watson, Robert, Jr. & Billie, Rt. 1, Box 711, Pittsboro  27312.....,..............542-4141
Watson, Elena, 419 Whitehead Cir...9...Potter.Tree.Rd.S.W...Rome.Ga.30.968-3921 301 6/
Watters, Carter, 210 Grimes, UNC-CH.................................................933-8728
Weaver, Robert P. & Catherina M., 79 Green Tree Tr.(Johanna).......................933-8682
Webb, Jane, Rt. 5, Box 393-A.......................................................933-7543
Webb, Louise, 2105 Carol Woods.....................................................929-2506
Webster, Patricia B., 716 Clearwater Lake Rd.(Ali).................................929-9865
Wedehase, Barbara, 103 Wild Turkey Tr.(Meghan, Brendan)............................942-2943
Weeber, Joy, 525 Hillsborough St., #5..............................................968-0393
Weikle, Timothy, 610 E. Rosemary St................................................933-0276
Weiss, Patricia, Rt. 4, Box 118.(C.T.).............................................929-6790
Weller, Ann, 869 Squire Ct., Cary  27511...........................................469-0833
Wells, Molly, 204 Brandywine.(Ryan, Jeffrey, Molly)................................967-5416
Wells, William, 803 Branch St......................................................929-9180
Werk, Stephen & Lynn, 8 Vauxhall Pl................................................493-8193
Wessner, Patricia F., 6 Country Club Circle, Brevard  28712........................885-8219
West-Hoffman, Shawn, Rt. 7, Box 148, Durham 27707..................................
Westerhoff, John & Alberta, 3510 Racine Dr., Durham  27707.........................493-1646
Weatneat, David & Susan, 24-A Stratford Hills Apts.................................967-9467
Weston-Dawkes, Jon & Sharon, 209-B Branson St......................................933-6667
Wheeler, Mary Lou, 604 Arlington St................................................942-5398
Wheeler, Eula, 28 Mt. Bolus Rd.....................................................967-7788
Whit, Nan, 412 Holly Ln.(Whitney)..................................................933-6336
Whitaker, Bethana, 134 Carol Woods.................................................942-2441
Whitcomb, Lee & Anne, 331 Fearrington Post, Pittsboro  27312.......................542-2766
White, David, PO Box 8, Carrboro 27510.............................................
White, Jess, 902 E. Franklin St., #5...............................................933-6892
White, Joe & Deborah, 309 Barclay Rd.(Seth)........................................933-9360
White, Mary Gray, 407 Patterson Pl.................................................967-7948
White, Molly, PO Box 2013, 27515.(211 Glenhill Ln).................................942-5739
Whitehurst, Deborah, 328 Burlage Circle............................................967-1982
Widmann, Frances, 1504 Cumberland Rd...............................................929-6581
Wiley, Dot, 412 W. Cameron Ave.....................................................942-3423
Wilkins, Charlie & Sandra, 201-D Estes Dr. Ext., Carrboro  27510.(Margaret).......967-7324
Williams, Andrea Jo, 1903 Ephesus Church Rd........................................967-4938
Williams, Andrea B., 413 Hillsborough St...........................................929-1307
Williams, Don, PO Box 570..........................................................967-7197
Williams, Elizabeth, 74 Laurel Ridge Apts..........................................967-2591
Williams, Jean: see LEUCHTENBURG, Jean
Williams, Randall & Elizabeth, 504 1-2 North St....................................929-3363
Williams, Stephen & Joanna, G-8 Village Green......................................967-4520
Williford, John & Heather, W-11 Old Well Apts., Carrboro  27510....................
Williford, Roy & Rita, 310 Coachway Dr.............................................967-0195
Willis, Park & Stephanie, 403 Colony Woods Dr.(Park, Laurie, Jed)..................967-5050
Wilroy, John & Emily, 149 Windsor Circle.(Mary Catherine, Joshua)..................942-8387
Wilson, Christine Love, 216 Westbrook Dr., Carrboro 27510..........................
Wilson, David & Lynn, 501 S. Fifth St., Mebane  27302..............................
Wilson, Frank & Anne, 603 Laurel Hill Rd...........................................942-4633
Wilson, John & Brenda, 854 Crosshill Rd., Danville, KY  40422......................
Wilson, Kay Smith, 1700 Ward St., Durham  27707....................................489-3200
Wilson, Nancy L.: see CORSE-WILSON, Nancy
Wilson, Peter, 500 North St........................................................942-1982
Windham, Albert & Eleanor, 434 Cameron Ave.........................................967-3506
Winfree, Derwood & Betty, 104 Oakstone Dr.(Colin, Anne)............................942-4544
Wing, Stafford & Janice, 1903 Overland Dr.(Claudia)................................929-1811
```

Witten, Sandra S.: see GRIFFIN, Sandra
Wofford, Adams, & Sibyl Wagner, 118 Village Ln.....................................967-0405
Wolfe, Walter & Jackie, Rt. 3, Box 495, Hillsborough 27278(Christopher,Stephanie)967-1367
Womack, Margaret, 3113 Carol Woods...967-1147
Woodgates, George & Sylvia, 200 Autumn Dr...942-6595
Woodiwiss, Ashley & Mary, 103 Dillard St., Carrboro 27510.........................929-3728
Woodland, Randy, 204 Friendly Ln..929-0077
Woodley, David & Christina, 195 Marilyn Lane.(Thatcher)...........................968-0732
Woodward, Mildred, 1304 Wildwood Dr...942-5037
Woodward, Henry & Enid, 2218 Carol Woods..967-7814
Wooten, Cecil, 14-C Sharon Heights Apts...967-7782
Working, Peter & Gerry, 1521 Arboretum Dr.(Katie, Meg)............................933-8311
Workman, Ann, 109 Hillcrest Ave., Carrboro 27510..................................933-7705
Worth, Alexander (Sandy), 209 Pritchard Ave.(William, Alexander)..................942-2421
Worth, Joan, 54-D Davie Circle...
Wortley, Rick & Kelly, 133 Brookberry Circle.......................................
Wright, Amanda, 716 Chateau Apts., Carrboro 27510.................................933-3111
Wright, Katherine, Buttons Ln...929-3532
Wright, Ben & Lydia, 407-B Smith Ave..967-1428
Wright, Robert, 110 Barbee Ct., Carrboro 27510....................................968-8083

- Y -

Yager, Dorne & Elise, 711 Emory Dr..929-3966
Yarborough, Margaretta Jane, PO Box 2035, 27515...................................967-7715
Yates, Jean Grote, Rt. 2, Box 516, Durham 27705.(Sheri, Laura)....................383-6934
Yeager, Bill & Gale, Rt. 1, Box 33, Morrisville 27560.(Willie)....................469-0019
Yegge, Vincent & Sarah, 1305 Quail Dr., Greensboro 27408..........................272-1636
Yeowell, David & Heather, 608 Concordia St.(Karen, Andrew, Angela)................967-5923
Yordy, Laura, 3101 Hope Valley Rd., Durham 27707..................................493-6206
Young, Jeff & Sharon, 1205 Willow Dr..942-0699
Young, Maria, 312 Cedar St..942-7058
Young, Ralph & Virginia, 739 Gimghoul Rd..942-0064
Young, Wiltsee & Carolyn, 1609 Old Oxford Rd.(Kathy Riley, Michelle Riley).......967-3861
Yount, William & Mary, 321 Reade Rd.(William, Christopher, Kathryn Mary)..........929-7444
Yow, Tere, 25 Bluff Tr..967-9695

- Z -

Zaragoza, Jay & Molly, 1432 Poinsett Dr.(Emlen, Elliott)..........................967-7720
Zdanski, Celeste, 706 N. Columbia St..929-1565
Zenger, Michael & Jeanine, 1109 Sourwood Circle (Peter)...........................929-6546
Ziff, Judith, 2621 Wells Ave., Raleigh 27608.......................................
Zunes, John & Helen, 161 Windsor Circle...942-6639

CPSIA information can be obtained
at www.ICGtesting.com
Printed in the USA
BVHW060925041218
534639BV00018BA/887/P